CATCH A TIGER BY THE TOE

ALSO BY ELLEN LEVINE

*The Journal of Jedediah Barstow: An Emigrant
on the Oregon Trail*

*Darkness over Denmark: The Danish Resistance
and the Rescue of the Jews*

*Freedom's Children: Young Civil Rights Activists
Tell Their Own Stories*

*A Fence Away from Freedom: Japanese Americans
and World War II*

Anna Pavlova: Genius of the Dance

CATCH
A
TIGER
BY
THE
TOE

by Ellen Levine

VIKING

VIKING
Published by Penguin Group
Penguin Young Readers Group, 345 Hudson Street, New York, New York 10014, U.S.A.
Penguin Group (Canada), 10 Alcorn Avenue, Toronto, Ontario, Canada M4V 3B2
(a division of Pearson Penguin Canada Inc.)
Penguin Books Ltd, 80 Strand, London WC2R 0RL, England
Penguin Ireland, 25 St Stephen's Green, Dublin 2, Ireland (a division of Penguin Books Ltd)
Penguin Group (Australia), 250 Camberwell Road, Camberwell, Victoria 3124, Australia
(a division of Pearson Australia Group Pty Ltd)
Penguin Books India Pvt Ltd, 11 Community Centre, Panchsheel Park, New Delhi –
110 017, India
Penguin Group (NZ), Cnr Airborne and Rosedale Roads, Albany, Auckland, New Zealand
(a division of Pearson New Zealand Ltd)
Penguin Books (South Africa) (Pty) Ltd, 24 Sturdee Avenue, Rosebank, Johannesburg 2196,
South Africa

Penguin Books Ltd, Registered Offices: 80 Strand, London WC2R 0RL, England

First published in 2005 by Viking, a division of Penguin Young Readers Group

10 9 8 7 6 5 4 3 2 1

LIBRARY OF CONGRESS CATALOGING-IN-PUBLICATION DATA
Levine, Ellen.
Catch a tiger by the toe / by Ellen Levine.
    p. cm.
Summary: In the Bronx, New York, during the McCarthy era, thirteen-year-old Jamie keeps
a terrible secret about her family, but when the truth is exposed, her parents lose their jobs
and she is fired from the school newspaper.
ISBN 0-670-88461-8 (hardcover)
[1. Toleration—Fiction. 2. Communism—Fiction. 3. Secrets—Fiction. 4. Schools—Fiction.
5. Family life—Bronx (New York, N.Y.)—Fiction. 6. Bronx (New York, N.Y.)—History—20th
century—Fiction. 7. United States—Politics and government—1945-1953—Fiction.]
I. Title. PZ7.L57833Cat 2005 [Fic]—dc22 2004017348

Printed in U.S.A.
Set in Fairfield
Book design by Sam Kim

FOR

Ide Gruber Levine,
Hannah Dorner Weinstein,
and Mary Elting Folsom

"*Restriction of free thought and free speech is the most dangerous of all subversions. It is the one un-American act that could most easily defeat us.*"   —*Supreme Court Justice William O. Douglas*

"*The House Un-American Activities Committee is the most un-American thing in America.*"   —*Harry S. Truman*

ALL I do is lie. Sometimes I think I'm the world-champion liar. Elaine is my almost-best friend, but I can't have a real one. How can I? It's one thing to lie to a teacher or a stranger, but to your best friend?

Someday I'm going to make a movie about lies: *The Bronx—1953, Worst Year of My Life.*

I mean, look what happened to Harriet Purdue. Her father's name was in the newspaper. They said he was a Communist, and he was fired from his job. They had to move out of the neighborhood. Kids avoided her. We were in gym together and shared a locker, but we weren't really friends.

I remember her last day clear as crystal. Not a single kid in gym said anything to her. Not even Myrna, her best friend. I didn't say anything either. It makes me nauseous to think about it. In the hallway it was the same thing. Everybody gave her lots of room, and nobody said a word. Then she was gone.

I wonder if Harriet's mad at her father.

I look normal, I think. Like any girl who's thirteen. Nothing special. Not red or blond hair. Just plain brown, which is good, because you don't want to stand out when you've got secrets. Stevie, my little brother, and my grandma also live with us. Uncle Maury lives four floors up in our apartment building. He's Mom's brother, so Stevie and I call them the M&Ms—Mom and Maury. Then there's Dad's brother, Uncle George. He and Aunt Sheila live a couple of blocks away. And that's it, my whole family.

"Remember, Jamie . . . zipped," Mom said when I came into the kitchen this morning. She's been saying that a lot more since what happened this summer. She pressed her lips together as if I didn't know to keep my mouth shut.

"Yeah, Mom, I know."

She looked at me and then out the window. "These are difficult times."

How could I forget? I'm so careful, lots of times I don't say anything. It's Stevie I worry about. He's not as good as I am at sliding out of tight spots—but he's only nine. I keep an eye on him. We aren't really lying, I've told him. We're heading people off. Diversion tactics, I call it.

When I was little, I used to love doing things with Mom and Dad. Lots of times I was the only kid with them and their friends at their rallies. But when I was about nine, the rallies stopped. I asked Mom why, but all she said was, "Things have changed." Like that really tells you something. But things *have* changed. When I pick up the newspapers at Mrs. Manny's candy store, she looks around before she hides the *Daily Worker* and the *National Guardian* inside the *New York Times* or the *Herald Tribune*. The first time she did that, she put her finger up to her lips and shook her head. When I told Dad, he said in a flat voice, "Politics."

I *hate* politics.

This afternoon a whole bunch of us were on the stoop outside the apartment building. School starts in two weeks, but everybody still has that summer feeling, hanging around, doing nothing. Me and Charlie Nathan were going to pick sides for a punchball game. Charlie's in my class and lives in our building four floors up. He's always going after somebody. Usually it's Herbie, a skinny kid with asthma, who lives on the first floor. Today Charlie was mouthing off about politics.

"The Legion's going after subversives," he said. "That's Commie-pinkos, Reds, just in case you don't understand big words like 'subversive.' You know, those guys trying to overthrow the government."

I've tried to think of a big word for Charlie. All I come up with is "jerk."

Charlie's father is in the American Legion, and every time I see Mr. Nathan he looks mad about something. It almost makes you feel sorry for Charlie. Almost.

"Hey, are we playing or not?" I started the count for who'd pick first.

"Eeny, meeny, miny, moe,
Catch a tiger by the toe.
If he hollers, let him go.
My mother says to pick the very best one.
Out goes Y-O-U."

I went back and forth between us without thinking.

Charlie looked at me. "Hey, Jamie, it's 'catch a nigger by the toe.'"

"Yeah, but it's a lot harder with a tiger!"

Charlie laughed. "You sure it ain't Commie talk?" He's so used to joking about everything being Commie this and Commie that, that he misses when he might be right.

There were eight of us. I picked two, Charlie picked three, and then I chose Herbie. For the first four innings, nothing much happened with him, except he struck out twice. But in the fifth, Herbie dropped an easy fly ball.

"Rubber fingers! Rubber fingers!" That's Charlie Nathan, always going after the weakest kid. Then, after the game, Herbie was trying to jump from the top step of the stoop. He couldn't seem to get up the nerve, and Charlie wouldn't let up.

"Hey! Hey, Herbie boy! I'm talking to you. Whattsa matter, legs too short?" So I jumped from the top step and accidentally-on-purpose butted into Charlie.

"Hey, Charlie, why don't you look where I'm coming?" Before he could figure that out, I walked off with Herbie to the playground.

Charlie likes to talk about Communists, but the other kids usually don't pay attention. I do. I just don't want to talk or hear about it. Usually Charlie leaves me alone. And I know it's because I won the American Legion citizenship award for my "I Am an American" school essay. Charlie's father was one of the Legion veterans onstage at the assembly when they gave me the plaque and a check for twenty-five dollars.

I'd never won anything before, and I thought it was really great to get money, but everybody went nuts. Mom wanted to tear the check up, Uncle Maury wanted to frame it, Dad said nothing, but Grandma said we should use it. "Better we spend it than the Legion has it." I agreed. We went out to dinner two Saturday nights on that check. And Grandma smiles sweetly whenever she sees Charlie.

2

"WANNA GO to the movies?"

It was Saturday and raining, and I figured Elaine would call. We go to the movies every Saturday we can and trade pictures of the stars. The movies are the safest place in the whole world. No politics, except for the newsreels, and you can't talk. You're away from everything.

Elaine always asks her mother when she sees the first raindrop. And then I can say she has permission when I ask Mom.

"Meet you at the candy store at noon," I told her.

I was sure Mom would let me go. Only ten days till school starts and maybe the last chance of the summer to go to the Palace Theater. She'd have to let me go.

"Mom, it's raining."

She gave me a why-are-you-telling-me-this look. We go through this every rainy Saturday. I don't know what she has against the movies.

"Elaine's mother said okay. Can I meet her? It's the new Esther Williams." That was a mistake.

"I've got a shopping list," she said as she wrote. Without looking up, she added, "Esther Williams and all those women swimming, kicking, spinning, ducking. It's a wonder they don't drown the way they keep their mouths open in those ridiculous smiles." That's my mom.

Yeah, well, if you were swept off a boat in a storm, you'd wish you could swim like Esther Williams. I didn't say that. Mom hates it when I "talk fresh." Instead I nodded. Joel McCrea in the second-feature western wouldn't help. I like him, but Mom's not interested in westerns either. Maybe I was adopted.

I waited. If the list wasn't too long, I could make it to the Palace on time. But almost everything she'd written was special, nothing normal like other families. "Can't we get the packaged pot cheese instead of from the crate?"

Mom sighed. I could see her weighing whether to ignore or answer. Ignore.

"White bread just for a change? Please, Mom? It's a lot faster. You know—doesn't have to be sliced."

"Take the list to Slonim's and Baumgarten's," she said in a tired voice. "If you're back in time, okay."

There was a line at both places, but the joke was, I was on time and Elaine was late. I waited under the candy store awning.

When I saw her round the corner, I yelled, "Hurry up! We'll miss Just Bill!" That's the newsreel rooster, and I love him. He crows in the middle of the screen as if he's saying, "Pay attention!" And then the announcer says, "Spanning the world!" and the news starts.

The minute you walk into the Palace, you know you're somewhere special—soft carpets and velvet-covered seats. If you carried me in when I was sound asleep and then woke me in the pitch-black darkness, I'd know I was at Loew's Palace. It's the smell of excitement—everybody waiting for the lights to turn off and the movie to start.

Elaine was puffing and turning red as she chugged up to me. She bent over panting. "My dad . . ." she gasped ". . . made me stick around. . . . He was reading me this article. . . ."

This wasn't going to be fun. I was there once when

her father read to us, and his face got red blotches all over. He was talking about some committee in Congress fighting the "Moscow Menace." A new red blotch popped up with each sentence. "Those damn Reds trying to take over the world!"—blotch on his forehead. "Got to get rid of the Commie traitors in our own government!"—blotch on his left cheek. I bet if he thought about it, he'd wish the blotches were a different color.

Dad talks a lot about politics, but no blotches, and he puts on his high school math-teacher voice, slow and steady. Elaine's father would probably look like his head was burned in a furnace if he ever met Dad. Her father thinks the Red-hunting committees in Congress are great. Mine says they are a menace, undermining the Constitution. Why does everybody have to talk about this stuff? Me and Elaine, we're like the heads and tails of the same penny. She's bored by politics. I hate it.

We ran to the Loew's Palace, Elaine puffing all the way. I was thinking about the whole day we'd be in there, but Elaine kept talking about her father. "He was real excited about President Eisenhower firing some man." She shrugged, as if irritated by a pesky fly.

That's Elaine. She doesn't care about the very thing that's my main secret. She probably wouldn't be my friend if she knew. Like the way everybody dropped Harriet. So I don't really count it as a big lie when I nod like I'm sort of agreeing with her.

We sat down just as the rooster crowed.

Elaine handed me her money. "Bon Bons," she said. Last time I saved the seats, and she went for the candy. Today I'm in a Three Musketeers mood. Esther Williams is on first. Then Joel McCrea in a western. What could be better?

We squinted like moles in the daylight when we got out. It was 5:30, and we'd been inside the Palace for five hours.

"I love the way Esther Williams looks happy all the time, even when she's underwater," Elaine said.

"Me too." And that was no lie. "When she leaps off the diving board with that big smile, you know nothing bad can happen."

We talked some more about the swimming girls and Joel McCrea. But Elaine went and spoiled it all. "I think I'll tell my father about the McCarthy stuff in the newsreel."

"Are you nuts? Why do you want to even bring that stuff up?"

"He'll smile like Esther." We both laughed. "Seriously, he'll be happy if he knows we're hearing about Senator McCarthy."

"Smart move," I said. But I sounded more cheerful

than I felt. Senator McCarthy, Senator McCarthy. That's all you hear about these days. Today in the newsreel, he was yelling about "communistic" books in American Embassy libraries in Europe.

"Thirty thousand books were written by Communists or their supporters," Elaine said.

I looked at her. "How'd you remember that? I thought you hated newsreels."

"I do, but that's some huge number. I can't picture it."

In the newsreel, Senator McCarthy had pushed back his chair, loosened his tie, and waved some papers in the air. "Roy Cohn," he said as he poked the man next to him, "he's my number-one aide, and he tells me these books are still staining the shelves of our overseas libraries."

"Those papers he had," I said, "I bet there's nothing on them." Actually I didn't think of that myself. It was Uncle Maury. He says it every time he sees a picture of Senator McCarthy.

"That's dumb," Elaine said. "Why would he say he's got a list if he doesn't?"

"Just because somebody says something, you believe them?"

"You're weird, Jamie. Don't you trust anybody?"

I laughed, but she was right.

"WHO'D BELIEVE it?" Mom was talking to herself when I walked past the table toward the front door. She looked at me and held up a clipping. "The Monogram movie studio canceled a film about Hiawatha."

When something in a newspaper or magazine tickles Mom, she clips it and leaves it for the week in the living room in her "Loony" file. Some articles, the ones she says have "staying power," get pasted into a scrapbook. And I have to admit, sometimes she finds really great stuff, like Just Bill, the movie rooster. He's from Kansas, and he won a contest to become the newsreel squawker because he could crow on cue.

"Want to help?" she asked, pointing to the glue jar.

"I'm meeting Elaine."

She waved the article over her head. "My smart daughter, pay attention. Hiawatha was a peacemaker, and talking about peace might, quote, 'aid the enemy,' unquote, according to this Hollywood producer." She jabbed at the clipping. "According to these people, you're a subversive if you care about peace."

I recited in a singsong voice,

"By the shores of Gitche Gumee,
By the shining Big-Sea-Water,
Stood the wigwam of Nokomis,
Daughter of the Moon, Nokomis."

Mom smiled.

"*Song of Hiawatha*," I said. "In fourth grade, they made us memorize part of that poem."

I love the name Gitche Gumee. It sounds like Indian chewing gum, but I know that's not what Mom's talking about. Politics is infecting everything. Even movies.

"How can you laugh about that stuff?" I said.

Mom looked surprised. I don't usually say anything when she talks about her political clippings. "Jamie, these are newspaper articles." She put down the paper. "You used to like the Loony file."

"Yeah, well, that was then."

It's true. I'd sit next to Mom and she'd read me stories from the paper. Loony always made Mom laugh. And when she laughed, so did I, even when I didn't understand. Once I laughed so hard I peed in my pants. When Stevie wanted to know what was so funny, "It's too hard to explain," I told him. The truth is, Mom's laugh is so rolling, you laugh along with her. But none of it seems funny after this summer.

She picked up the clipping again. "This one's got staying power," she said, as she reached for the glue jar.

"I'm going to the playground."

It's late summer and still light out. School starts in a little over a week, Senator McCarthy is all over the news "hunting down Reds," and Mom's cutting and pasting in her scrapbook. I left.

I met Elaine in the playground, and we watched the boys play basketball until we got tired. I can never figure out why you get so tired doing nothing, but we were yawning like crazy.

"Hey, come on, Jamie. Let's go back to your house."

Here's what I mean about not having a real best friend. I've been to Elaine's apartment, but she's never been to mine. I've always managed to come up with a good excuse, but today she really pressed me. I shook my head. I mean, who knows what someone might talk about.

"Not fair. We always go to mine."

"Can't."

"Why not?"

I took a deep breath. "Because my grandma lives with us and she's very sick and very weak, and she needs total quiet and everybody walks around in socks, and much as I'd love you to come over it's impossible."

Which of course is ridiculous. People come over all the time. Uncle George and Aunt Sheila and Uncle Maury. Uncle Maury doesn't wear socks, but he does wear fuzzy slippers. That's because he lives upstairs, not because he's trying to be quiet. And not only relatives. Plenty of people Dad and Mom know come over. And although Grandma is very old, she's got all her marbles.

If Elaine did come over, she'd probably see Grandma sitting in the living room at a card table, peeling potatoes or apples, or slicing carrots, or chopping onions, or folding laundry. She's always doing something.

"Don't you ever take a break?" I once asked her.

"This is nothing compared to the Old Country," she said. I love it when she tells us stories about Russia when she was a young girl. I know Elaine would like the stories too. But I've made Grandma "really really sick," so that's the end of Elaine coming over.

Another thing I haven't told Elaine about is the movies I make up in my head. I don't remember when I started, but if you don't have somebody to talk to, you can put all that untalked talk in a movie you make up. MMM, I call my studio: Movies in the Mind by Morse. They're my movies. I write the scripts, pick the characters, direct them, and best of all—absolutely the best of all—if I don't like the ending, I can change it.

Maybe the biggest thing I'd never tell Elaine is, I'm afraid of the F.B.I.

I KNEW the minute those two men started coming toward me, they were F.B.I. Maybe it was the way they glanced back and forth across the street. Maybe it was the way they had their hands in their pockets. I don't know, I just knew.

"Hey, Jamie Morse." The one who spoke took off his hat and peered down at me. The other one took out a pad and started writing even before I said anything.

How did he know my name? Right away that was scary. I must have nodded without thinking because Mr. Talker went on.

"Okay, Jamie, we just want to ask you a few questions. Real easy ones." He looked at his partner, then back to me. "It's a survey about newspapers we're doing. Does your Dad read the *New York Times*? The *National Guardian*? The *Daily Worker*?"

Did he think Mom didn't read? Did he think he could trick me? "The *Journal American*," I said. That was a whopper. The *Journal American*, Mom says, is very conservative. She says it would "besmirch" our home to buy it. And that's why we don't get to read the *Journal* comics, which are really good, unless we're at somebody else's house.

These men must have thought I was real dumb. Sure, they're doing a questionnaire. My foot!

"My foot!" I said. I startled myself as well as them. I ran around Mr. Talker, up the block, and headed for the playground. I wasn't going home with them following me.

Then I thought about it. If they knew my name, I'm sure they know what building we live in, even what apartment.

The first time I heard about the F.B.I., I must have been about seven. Dad and Grandma had taken me with them to a "Wallace for President" rally at Madison Square Garden. Mom stayed home with Stevie. He was only a little kid, not old enough to come with us.

I'd never been in such a gigantic place with so many people. Dad said everyone had come to celebrate, because a very good man was running for president. Mr. Wallace supported "the little people," people who work hard and don't make a lot of money, Dad said, and so we supported him. Grandma, Dad, and I sat pretty high up. I couldn't understand most of the speakers, but whenever Grandma cheered, I cheered. Dad isn't much of a noisemaker. When he likes something, he nods. But that night Grandma and me, well, we were loud enough for the three of us. Everybody around us was smiling and talking, and I felt happy.

When we left, Dad was holding my right hand, Grandma my left. Suddenly Grandma pulled me in tight to her side and started hollering, "*Cossacks! Cossacks!*" at two men who were taking pictures of everybody. Dad pulled his hat down, but Grandma, she just hollered, shaking her fist first at one, then the other.

On the subway going home, nobody said a word for at least five station stops. I was too frightened to ask anything, and they each seemed to have forgotten I was there. Finally I asked Dad for a tissue. He looked startled, as if he had just remembered something. Me. Then he explained that Grandma hated police who spy on you, like the F.B.I. When she lived in Russia, he said, they were called the czar's Third Section and Cossack raiders.

"All men on horseback," I remember Grandma saying.

A few days after that, Mom and Uncle Maury were in the living room talking, and I was on the floor with Stevie, teaching him the alphabet.

Mom said, "They should be hunting criminals, not us."

Who was she talking about?

Uncle Maury started pacing. "They snoop on meetings that are perfectly legal. None of their damn business!"

"Who?" I said.

"The F.B.I. with its foot on our throat. Bah!" Uncle Maury shook his head in disgust.

"They hate us?" I asked.

"You could say that," he said.

Stevie pulled at my sleeve. "What's after H-I-J?"

"F-B-I," I said.

Mom looked up. "Time for bed." She took Stevie into his room and sent me into mine.

"What is the F.B.I.?" I asked when she came in.

She straightened my blanket.

"Why does it hate us?" I pressed.

"F.B.I. stands for Federal Bureau of Investigation. It's the police force for the government."

"Why do they hate us?"

"We'll talk about it tomorrow, Jamie."

"Could they do something bad to us?" I can still feel Mom squeezing my hands tight.

"Could they do something bad?" I repeated.

"Sweetheart, don't worry. You have to be careful, that's all."

"Careful about what?"

"Well." She paused. "If a stranger asks you questions, just say, 'Excuse me, sir, but I have to go home now.'"

"What kinds of questions?"

Mom didn't answer right away. When she did, I shivered, and I've never forgotten what she said. "Anything about your family. About me and Daddy, or Uncle Maury, or Uncle George." She put her arm around me. "It's really a simple rule. Don't talk to strangers. Your mouth is zipped up, like this." She pinched her fingers and drew a line across her lips. "And this is very important. If someone you don't know comes to the door"—she said, speaking each word as if it were a whole sentence—"don't . . . let . . . them . . . in. Don't . . . say . . . anything." I stared at her. "The same for the telephone. If anyone you don't know calls, hang up."

I wanted to pull the covers over my head.

"But don't worry," she said in a cheerful voice. "Everything will be fine."

Everything will be fine?

From that day on I've been very careful about strangers. For a couple of years until I was about nine, I still had to ask people to cross me at the stop light, but that was it, just "Mister, can you cross me?" Ever since then, I've been on the watch. And nobody has ever asked me any questions.

Until today, that is.

"Some F.B.I. men asked me questions," I said. Uncle Maury ate with us, and I tried to focus on his fuzzy slippers. Under the right foot there's a hole the size of a quarter. But everybody kept asking me over and over again about the men, and each time I repeated the story.

The fourth time Stevie said, "You already told that."

Finally Uncle Maury stopped it. "Leave the kid alone."

Uncle George and Aunt Sheila arrived just as Grandma went to heat the apple strudel. This is not the first time that's happened. I think Uncle George times it so he gets here for dessert. Tonight his eyes flicked over to the kitchen, waiting for the strudel, I'm sure. Slinky eyeballs, Stevie calls him.

Uncle George and Uncle Maury don't really like each other. They're always disagreeing about Russia. Once when they were arguing, Uncle Maury sneezed and Uncle George hollered, *"Polluter!"* Mom cracked up, and I laughed so hard I got a pain in my stomach.

There was no laughing tonight.

"The F.B.I. interrogated her," Uncle Maury said, nodding toward me.

"The F.B.I.?" Uncle George bellowed.

"Could they arrest Jamie if they knew she was lying?" Stevie's question cut through the noise.

Dad fiddled with his spoon for an endless minute. "Nobody's getting arrested, but it's not good to lie."

"It's either silence or lies," Uncle Maury said. "And sometimes it's better to lie." Sometimes I wish Uncle Maury was my dad.

Tapping his spoon, that's what Dad was doing. Just tapping.

"Don't you see? I have to lie." I looked at Dad. "I have to lie, and it's your fault!"

I ran out, slamming the door.

Down the stairs, three flights. Out of the building, down the stoop. Seven—five—three—one—sidewalk. Out! Kids were playing punchball in the parking lot. Charlie was hunched against the factory wall across the street. Looked like he'd been crying. Charlie crying? Can't be. Barry waved. I pretended not to see.

The Crazy Lady was walking up the block. I crossed quickly to the other side of the street. I don't want to think about her. Keep walking.

"If Vesuvius erupted, they'd all be buried with their mouths open in hollering position. I can't stand it!" I hear my voice. Out loud, like the Crazy Lady.

Who is she, anyway? She has to live in one of the buildings around here, because I see her all the time. She always wears the same house dress. Gray, with a faded flower print, and she carries a shopping bag. Some kids say she smells, but I've never been close enough to tell. She walks as if she has no end in mind. She mumbles to herself, and her hair covers most of her face. Does she think nobody can see her?

"WHERE'D YOU go?" Stevie asked me in the morning. He was sticking Cheerios on toothpicks and standing them up on a piece of toast. His cereal bowl, half empty, was on the table.

"Out. Mom won't appreciate that mess, you know. Where is she, anyway?" I asked.

"It's Tuesday, dumbo. She's getting stuff for an apple pie."

"Dad?"

"He left with her." Stevie went back to toothpicking. Tuesday is Mom's day off from the radio station where she writes for *The Fettleson Family* show. And every Tuesday night our whole family sits in the living room to listen when it comes on.

"Apple pie, that's good. Those burnt oatmeal cookies last week were awful," I said.

"Yeah, we should've gone to Mrs. Baumgarten's."

I left and hung out on the stoop. After a while Stevie came down. He was holding a small box. "I didn't know Uncle Joe got the Purple Heart," he said.

"Let me see that." I took the box and opened it. Next to the medal was a paper with Dad's writing on it: "Joe. August 12, 1944." We didn't know much about Uncle Joe. Just that he had driven an ambulance in France during the war. He'd died over there, and Dad would never talk about him or the war.

"Found it in a carton in the front closet." Stevie took back the box. "Maybe before the show starts we can ask."

I left him and walked to the candy store. The new Archie comics were in. If you stood with your back to the counter and there were other people there, you could sometimes read them before Mr. McGinnis caught you. The candy store and Elaine's were the only places I got to read comics. Mom didn't let us buy them. I got through one Archie and headed for the playground. Elaine and I said we'd meet in the afternoon after her piano lesson.

✦ ✦ ✦

By the time I got home, Mom was working hard. She had pans and bowls and wooden spoons on every counter.

Uncle Maury leaned against the kitchen doorframe. "How can someone with such an orderly, rigorous mind make such a mess?" he said.

Mom had her hands in the dough bowl. "Analysis I don't need. Hand me the tin of walnuts." She nodded toward the pantry, and flour dust that had settled in her hair drifted down around her face.

"At least everything smells good," Uncle Maury said.

Mom was pouring tablespoons of something into the mixing bowl. Stevie came into the kitchen with the Purple Heart box. "When did Uncle Joe get the Purple Heart?" he said. Mom pushed a lock of hair behind her ear. She was in a cloud of flour. "Later, Stevie. I'll lose count."

I turned to leave.

"How many tablespoons have I put in?"

"It's show night. Cheer up!" Uncle Maury ruffled my hair as I passed him.

Grandma was in the living room and motioned me to follow her. In her room was a box from Baumgarten's Bakery. "Insurance," she said with a smile.

I gave her a hug. "I'm glad you live with us."

＋ ＋ ＋

Actually, I like that Mom writes for the Fettleson show. It's one of the most popular programs on the air. Elaine's whole family tunes in every Tuesday night, and they're not the only ones. I think all of New York listens. In fact that's how Elaine and I became friends. I never say anything about my family, even things that are okay. I figure if I don't say anything, I'll never slip. So I must have been half-asleep the day Elaine asked me if Mom stayed at home. "No," I said. "She writes stories for the Fettleson show."

Elaine got so excited, she screamed, "You're kidding! I never thought about somebody writing the stories."

"Yeah, well, she writes some of them."

"You mean it? . . . Really? . . . Cross your heart?"

"I wouldn't make up something like that," I said, knowing, of course, I could have.

Elaine grinned. "It's my favorite show!"

I smiled back. But I'd broken my tell-nothing rule, and it made me nervous. "You can't tell anybody," I told her. And I made up a story about an evil aunt who was searching for my mom, and since you never knew who might say something, even accidentally, and reveal our whereabouts, she had to swear to never, cross-her-heart-and-hope-to-die, ever breathe a word of this to anybody.

"But I don't know anybody."

"You've got to promise. I'm telling you, it's an absolutely, positively serious danger."

She was disappointed she couldn't say she knew somebody famous, but she promised. Now, every week Elaine wants to know if Mom has written that week's show. Mom's not the only writer, of course, but we know when her shows are on, unless the station makes a last-minute change. So usually I can tell Elaine in advance.

Tuesday nights after dinner we're all in the living room. Grandma turns the sound up loud. She doesn't let you move for the whole half hour. Stevie once brought in a coloring book and crayons, and Grandma made him put it away. "Pay attention and watch, so you don't miss your mama's story." Stevie stared at the radio for the whole time. I think he actually thought he'd see something.

We always eat early on Tuesdays. That way Grandma says we can take our time getting comfortable. Everybody's got their favorite place. Dad's in the big living-room chair, the throne we call it. Mom's on the right arm of the couch, Grandma's smack in the middle of the couch, and Uncle Maury opens a folding chair. Stevie lies on the rug right in front of the radio. I change places every week.

"And tonight's theme is . . . ?" Uncle Maury asked Mom.

"Mr. Carbo and Mr. Ribset fighting over the best breading for a veal chop," she said. "And that's all I'm saying."

"They're my favorites," I said to Grandma. She agreed. Mr. Carbo is a grouchy grocer who really wants to be a baker, and Mr. Ribset is the man who had to be a butcher with a name like that. They are always trying to outsmart Mrs. Fettleson, and of course they always lose. "Hey, Mom, can't you ever let them win over Mrs. Fettleson?"

"Not on your life. Tuna fish casserole coming up."

As if it could be anything else. Every Tuesday night we have tuna casserole with crumbled potato chips on top. With my whole family, you know what's happening by what they eat and where they sit.

"So what western did you see Saturday?" Uncle Maury asked me.

Stevie looked up. "How'd you know she went to the movies and saw a western?"

"Elementary, my dear Watson. It was Saturday, it was raining, and there's almost always a cowboy movie on the double bill in the summer."

"*Lone Hand*, with Joel McCrea. There's this secret outlaw gang that controls the whole territory, and the government wants to catch them."

All the grown-ups looked up.

"It's about this cowboy, Joel McCrea, who's riding with a band of outlaws. When his son finds out, he's so upset he won't even look at McCrea. But McCrea is secretly working for the law. He's really an under-cover agent for the government."

Dad raised his fork like a blackboard pointer. "The cowboy version of the F.B.I.," he said. "What will they think of next?"

You have to understand, in my house almost nobody is lower than an F.B.I. informer. And it's all because of Senator McCarthy and those committees in Congress. They say the Communists are trying to overthrow the government, so it's your patriotic duty to give the name of every Communist you know. Dad says some people are so scared of losing their jobs, they're giving the committees the names of their friends. Even though Dad and Mom and Uncle Maury and Uncle George don't agree about a lot of political stuff, they all say anybody who turns on their friends is as low as a rat.

"Maybe this is different," I said. "These were out-laws stealing cattle and robbing banks and killing people." My face felt hot. "Maybe it's not the same kind of rat."

Dad poured himself some water. "Maybe they are different, Jamie. But these days everything is about symbols. If, in the movies, the hero turns in people to the government, everybody sees that as a good thing to do."

"They're cowboys," I insisted, "but because of you I couldn't even see this movie without thinking about rats and stool pigeons."

"Jamie," Mom said. "Stop it. This minute."

I pushed my plate away.

"Can I have your potato chips?" Stevie said.

"Who cares." I pushed the plate farther. But I couldn't stop. "I mean, Mr. Carbo and Mr. Ribset and Mrs. Fettleson. They're silly. Why can't I like something silly?"

Nobody said a word.

"Good question, Jamie," Uncle Maury said finally. "And I say, don't give away your potato chips or the casserole for that matter. You need a full stomach to listen to the Fettlesons."

I went into my room. A little later Stevie came in.

"Barry banged five times on the pipe," he said.

Barry lives below us, and we use the kitchen pipe like a walkie-talkie. Five knocks is *meet-me-on-the-stoop*. No way I was going to go out now. "Knock three times for me, okay?"

Stevie grinned. "That's *I-can't-come*, right? I did already. We have to ask Uncle Maury about the Purple Heart before the show starts."

✦   ✦   ✦

"Uncle Maury," Stevie said, "we didn't know Uncle Joe had gotten a Purple Heart." Dad turned when he heard Uncle Joe's name, but then looked away.

Stevie held the medal cupped in his hands, as if it were alive. "Did he get it 'cause he died?"

Uncle Maury took the box from Stevie and stared at the medal. "It's awarded to any member of the armed forces killed or wounded in action." He handed the box back to Stevie. "When the war started, we went over together. Your uncle Joe was a medic. He didn't want to be part of the killing, he said." Uncle Maury closed his eyes and rubbed his forehead. Uncle Joe had died, and Uncle Maury had come home. That much we knew.

"I wish I had known him," I said.

Uncle Maury reached out and took my hand. "He was tall, you're short. He wasn't pretty like you, definitely not," he laughed. "But one thing's the same—you both ask lots of questions."

"I bet he wasn't scared much," I said.

Uncle Maury looked at me. "Something bothering you, Jamie?"

I shrugged.

Stevie looked down at the medal in his hand. He traced George Washington's picture with his finger. "I guess I'll never get to fight the bad guys."

"Don't worry. There are always bad guys to fight," Uncle Maury said.

Grandma had been listening. "In this country, we fight when we vote." She tapped Stevie on the chest with her finger. "You come in the booth with me next time. You too," she said to me.

Somehow when Grandma tries to teach a lesson, she never makes you feel dumb. Like you should have already known something and why should she have to waste time telling you.

Uncle Maury got up to move near the radio. We followed him.

School starts tomorrow.

Big open camera angle on the schoolyard. Kids are out for recess. "Who's that?" Charlie Nathan yells to somebody outside the fence. The camera pulls back to show me walking with this incredibly handsome soldier. I smile a very small smile and take the soldier's hand. We keep on walking. Past the school. Past the school-yard. "Who was that?" the soldier asks. "Nobody in particular," I say.

EVERYONE SAYS Mr. Tubell dyes his mustache. Is that lying? I have him for homeroom this year because I'm on the school paper, and he's the paper's adviser. I've wanted to be on the paper ever since I can remember. We had to submit a writing sample for a tryout, so I guess my history report on the Boston Tea Party was good enough.

Herman's News Breaks is the official name of the paper, but everybody calls it *NB*. I don't know anybody who knows who Herman was, but the school's named after him. Anyway, I heard Mr. Tubell gets the whole staff in a circle when he's ready to send everything off to the printer, and says, "All right people, not bad." I just figured out that's also *NB*.

I know Mr. Tubell from last year. He was my science teacher, and he always had something smelly in a jar in the back of the room by the sink. The worst was the frog heart preserved in formaldehyde.

"Bountiful biology," he called it. "This is the process of life." But the frog was dead. Nobody should be allowed to stare into somebody's heart like that.

Mr. Tubell loved to surprise us. He'd mix two clear chemicals. "Challenging chemistry, people," he'd say. He always called us "people." Made you feel older.

"Look through the jars, people. What do you see?"

We stared at the clear liquid in each jar right through to the back sink.

"The sink," we said, waiting for the magic moment.

"And what color is it?"

"Stainless steel," someone joked. The rest of us groaned.

Mr. Tubell took an eye dropper and twirled it between his fingers. He turned the jar cap so you heard every twist. We stared as the tip of the dropper sucked up the chemical from one jar. Slowly he lowered the dropper into jar number two and squirted.

"Voilà! And now what color is number two?"

"Blue!" We stared at the color oozing through the

liquid until jar number two was a totally new color. How could one clear liquid turn another clear liquid blue? Mr. Tubell always explained the chemical interactions, but still it felt like magic.

"Just a little input from a new force," he'd say, "and look what you can do, yes?"

He reminded me of Grandma. That's how she talks about politics. "A little input, my darling," she says, "to make such a change so everybody should have three good meals and a roof over the head."

Now I'm in the *NB* homeroom with Mr. Tubell, but without test tubes. "All right, people," he said, "here's a style sheet." He handed a pile of papers to the boy in the first row, front seat. "Pass these out, Clifford. Thanks."

That's another thing. Mr. Tubell is the only teacher I've ever had who says, "Thank you."

"Look at item number four, people." Mr. Tubell held up the sheet. "I'm always asked about it, so I'm heading you off at the pass." He sounded like Joel McCrea.

"All articles are to be typed," Mr. Tubell read. "At the bottom of every page, type the word 'more.'" He looked up at us. "That way the editors and I know more is coming. Simple?" We all laughed. He read on. "At the end of the article, on your last page, type a dash, space, the number thirty, space, and another dash." He drew it on the board: - 30 -. "Don't ask me why it's thirty. I don't know." Mr. Tubell is also the only teacher who says when he doesn't know something.

"I need a volunteer to organize last year's files. Any takers?" Iris Fleming and I raised our hands. "Fine, Jamie," Mr. Tubell said.

The bell rang, and everyone filed out. "Jamie," he said, as he motioned to me to come up to his desk. "Glad to see you're someone who gets involved."

Boy, was he wrong. I almost never volunteer. *Don't be the nail that sticks up*, is my motto. Which means if you do volunteer for something easy, people don't notice when you duck down other times.

"Stop by after your last class, and I'll show you the files."

I nodded. First homeroom day. I'm on *NB*, and everything's okay so far.

"Come over later?" Elaine asked, when we met at the lockers. "I got the new *Modern Screen*." That's her favorite movie magazine. I like them all.

"Okay, I just have to check in with Mr. Tubell first."

She was bending down to get her gym bag when she said, "He's really cute, don't you think? And so smart."

I stared at her. "Who?"

"Paul, jerko. But I don't know, he's so serious."

I pictured Paul Shapiro contradicting some dumb thing someone said last year in social studies. "He's not afraid of anybody," I said. "I bet he never lies about anything."

"Who's talking about lies?" Elaine asked. "You really are weird sometimes, Jamie."

I was going through my fifth *Modern Screen*. "Gregory Peck," I said, looking up. We'd been talking favorites for most of the afternoon. "I mean, take *Roman Holiday*. How could Audrey Hepburn go back to being a princess, when she could have married Gregory Peck?"

Elaine chewed her nail. "Maybe that's why it's called *Roman Holiday*, not *Roman Wife*."

"He's my all-time-absolute-forever-and-ever favorite. Tingles your hands to look at him."

She nodded. "Okay, he's a tingly-hand." Then in a real low voice she said, "Paul is a tiny tingle."

I stared at her. "*A tiny tingle?* You must be kidding. The boys in our class are so . . . so—"

"So what?"

"I don't know, so . . . so . . . boy."

"Same age as us."

"That's what I mean. And, besides, dumb."

She snorted. "The one thing Paul isn't, is dumb."

I shrugged and flipped the pages of *Screen Album*. "Gregory Peck is gorgeous." I challenged her. "You can't name one boy you've ever seen in the whole school who's gorgeous like that." Elaine kept on cutting. But she was smiling.

Nothing was going to spoil this afternoon. Mom doesn't let me buy movie magazines. Elaine has a closetful of them, and I was sitting on the floor in the middle of a mountain of stories and pictures of Hollywood's movie stars. The best.

"Oh, wow," I yelled. "Here it is!" I held open two pages in *Photoplay*. *From Here to Eternity,* with Burt Lancaster and Deborah Kerr kissing on the beach with the waves coming in and washing over them. That was the most hand-tingly thing I'd ever seen. Elaine had been looking for this picture for her scrapbook section on great love scenes. I passed it over to her. Funny. Like Mom, Elaine is a clipper. But much better stuff.

"Wouldn't you give anything to look like Deborah Kerr?" she said.

"Freckles." I pointed to my nose. "Hopeless."

Elaine nodded sympathetically. "But they're cute on Paul," she murmured.

I stared at her. "What's happening to you, Elaine? Van Johnson," I said, pointing to a *Movie World* cover. *"That's* cute."

"Just forget it, okay?" She went back to cutting. Me, to reading.

After a while everything got peaceful again. "Listen,

Jamie, next week I'm going to exchange a pile of old *Photoplay*s and *Modern Screen*s with Sandy Cooper. We haven't decided what day yet. Wanna come?"

"I'm not sure I can." I always say something like that to give myself time to think. But what bad could happen from loving Gregory Peck? Maybe I'll go.

"HEY, DAD, I'm on the paper this year." The DO NOT DISTURB sign was up, but sometimes I do anyway, like an itch you scratch when you shouldn't. Dad kept on reading. Maybe he didn't hear me.

"I'm on the *NB* staff this year, Dad. I really wanted to make the paper. Remember?"

He looked up and nodded. "Excellent."

"Yeah, it'll be fun."

He put down the paper he was reading. "A newspaper, Jamie, can be a source of truth and a source of lies." Then he went back to reading.

"Dad, this is *NB*, not AP. You know, kids."

"Good," he said. "Maybe you'll write about something more important than the Halloween costume party."

I stared at him. My nails dug into my palms. "Maybe if I said some union had a rally outside and there was a picket line—"

Grandma put down the potato peeler and came over to me. She put her arm through mine. "It's good to be a newspaper reporter," she said quietly, and walked me to my room. She sat on my bed while I walked the three steps from my desk to the bureau, round and round, back and forth.

"Dad reads about politics, Mom clips. Do they care more about that than us?" I struggled to keep from crying. "Why can't they be like normal people?"

Stevie came in and sat down next to Grandma. They both looked at me.

"I mean, I'm glad they raised money for the Stillwells when they couldn't pay their rent, and I did yell at Charlie when he called Annie Mae Jordan a nigger behind her back, and it was really terrible because I know she heard him, and I know everybody should have three good meals a day, and I think Paul Shapiro is great when he answers Mrs. Ridit in social studies class, and . . . and . . . and I hate myself that I can't do that. . . ."

I started to tremble.

"Can't we once, just once, sit down to dinner, and nobody says anything except 'Pass the butter, please,' or 'The meat loaf is really good,' or 'How nice you're on the newspaper staff'"—I paused—"without one word about the president or Congress or Senator McCarthy or anything about politics?"

"But all Daddy said was something about Halloween."

I stared at Stevie. Grandma pulled me over and put her arms around me.

"Politics is not such a terrible thing, my sweetheart," she said. "It brought us here, and because of that your mama is an American and you are an American."

"So what's so great about that?" I said into her shoulder.

"I'll tell you," she said quietly. "In the middle of a dark night almost forty years ago," she began, "Papa and I crept out of Minsk with nothing but our false identity papers. We wanted to come to a free country."

"That's not what I'm talking about, Grandma. That's not now. Can't you understand? It's not about back then." I started to pull away.

"Jamele, I am not only talking about Papa's and my story. It's your story too. Yesterday is always today."

"Russia is not my story," I said. My shoulders were as tight as a knot.

But Grandma went on. "There was no democracy

in Russia when Papa and I lived there. The czar was the emperor of Russia, and he had absolute power. At his word, people lived or died. Papa was hiding from the czar's men. They were going to force him, like many young Jewish men, into the Russian army for twenty-five years. So he had to run away."

"And you wouldn't let him go alone," Stevie said.

Grandma nodded. "Leib Nochomovsky was a brilliant artist," she said. "He made us our new identity cards. You'd have to be some kind of devil to see they weren't real. And of course we had a new name, Fyodorovich. I was Katya and Papa was Mikhail. With such names, who could possibly guess we were Jewish?"

Secrets. I listened in spite of myself. I don't know if it was Grandma's voice or the story I'd heard so many times, but I began to relax.

"This was before the great Russian Revolution, and we were here in America when the news came of the downfall of the czar."

"Grandma, did you ever see the czar?" Stevie asked.

"I have never told you about the czar's carriage?"

"Tell," I whispered.

She pulled us both closer. "I was in Saint Petersburg visiting my cousin Masha. She worked in a small bookshop off Nevsky Prospect. One morning we were moving boxes of books from the cellar upstairs to the shelves, when we heard a great commotion in the street. Outside a crowd had gathered. Someone shouted, 'The czar is coming! The czar is coming.' Soon everyone was crying, 'The czar, the czar!'

"He arrived in a carriage so sparkling, diamonds you knew were the door handles. A black-and-gold carriage drawn by four white horses with feathered plumes," Grandma said, peering as if she could see all the way back to St. Petersburg.

"Suddenly an old man in a ragged coat ran into the street. He had a piece of paper in his hand and he offered it to the czar, who was waving out the carriage window. The royal coachman raised his whip and struck the old man. The poor soul only wanted to give the czar a note. Whipped," Grandma said bitterly. "The old man fell beneath the wheels and was crushed." Grandma twisted her hands in her lap. "The czar pulled down the carriage shades and rode on. Never looked back."

The three of us sat very still.

"So you see, I would have danced in the streets if I had been there when the czar was overthrown."

"But you were here in New York," I said.

"We were here in New York. And Papa looked at me, and I looked at him, and we knew it was time to get rid of Katya and Mikhail Fyodorovich. I don't know why we didn't think of it before, but the time was right, down with the czar, down with Fyodorovich."

"And back to Itskowitz," Stevie said. "But Itskowitz is too hard for people to spell." Stevie loved saying Itskowitz.

"You remember everything," Grandma said. "Yes, and that's how your mama came to be born Rachel Israel and not Itskowitz."

Grandma leaned back. "We hoped for so much with the Russian Revolution. Not only workers and peasants, we thought, but also Jews for the very first time were going to be free in this new Soviet Union to have a decent roof over their heads . . ."

". . . and three good meals," Stevie and I both said.

"And three good meals, yes. And much good happened, but now, now, not so good. Stalin is the new dictator in Russia. Like the czar, he rules with an iron hand."

"What's that mean?" Stevie said.

"He makes all the laws. If you question, you go to prison or maybe you are killed."

"Why do good things turn bad, Grandma?" I said.

"I don't know, sweetheart. I don't know."

The three of us sat quietly.

"Does it have to be like that?" Stevie said.

"I hope not." Grandma stood up and headed for

her room. "I want to show you something.

"Be very careful," she said when she came back. "This is precious to me." She held out an envelope.

I took it in both hands and lowered it to the rug as gently as if it were a baby. Inside were newspaper clippings. The first one was from the *New York Times*, March 16, 1917. The headline read:

REVOLUTION IN RUSSIA
CZAR ABDICATES

"What's that mean?" Stevie asked.

"Gave up being czar," I said quickly. I wanted to read on.

Grandma pointed to the fourth paragraph. "Start there," she said. "Petrograd—that's Saint Petersburg," Grandma explained.

> Petrograd has been the scene of one of the most remarkable risings in history, beginning with minor food riots and labor strikes last week Thursday. The people's cry for food reached the hearts of the soldiers, and one by one the regiments rebelled, until finally those troops which had for a time stood loyal to the Government gathered up their arms and marched into the ranks of the revolutionists.

Grandma touched my arm. When I looked up, her eyes glowed. And I saw how beautiful she must have been when she was a young woman.

"When the troops were ordered to fire on the people marching in the streets, they refused. Refused! Now read that," she said, as she pointed to a faded line of ink next to a paragraph farther down the page. "It is the words of the president of the Duma, the Russian parliament, when he saw the masses of people in the streets."

I bent down close to the paper to read the small type.

> President Rodzianko, who presided, sent a telegram to the Emperor, informing him of the developments and calling on him to listen to the voice of the people. "The hour has struck," he said, "when the will of the people must prevail."

"The will of the people must prevail," Grandma repeated softly. "He spoke our dreams."

Stevie stared at the clipping. "It's in a newspaper, not in a social studies book," he said. "It's real. Like it happened yesterday."

Grandma cleared her throat. "So you see some newspaper stories are important."

I didn't look up, but I knew she was talking to me.

"Your father is a decent man, a good man," she said. "It is a hard time now. Your parents, they worry. They worry for all of us."

"Could Dad lose his job?" I said in a low voice. "Or Mom?"

Grandma pulled us closer. "*S'vetzik oispressen*," she said in Yiddish. "It will press itself out." I wanted her to be right. I wanted to believe that everything would be okay.

I leaned in closer to her. Mom and Uncle Maury must have grown up hearing bedtime stories from Grandma about Russia and the revolution. With Grandma I don't mind politics. When she tells us stories, they're about family, and you can picture them happening.

I remembered Mom's good family stories, and how I used to make her repeat over and over the one about when she and Dad met and fell in love. She'd always laugh when she told it. "There I was at this dance, and this really good-looking fella came up to me. The strangest thing was, he started to speak, but no words came out. I stared right at him and said as sharply as I could, 'Yes?' He blinked and then asked me if I'd like to go with him the following Thursday night to a concert."

At that point Stevie and I always said ". . . And you

talked all night and into the morning, and the rest is history."

"You know it's true, Pete," Mom would say if Dad was there. "Don't be embarrassed. You were very shy, and I thought it was sweet."

Whenever Mom said politics brought them together, Uncle Maury would laugh. "Politics, schmolitics. Your father liked the way she danced the Peabody!"

I wish I knew them back then. It sounds like they had a lot of fun. Once, a couple of years ago, I got them to show me the Peabody. They had to move all the chairs in the living room and push the sofa against the wall. They swooped out from each other and back again, holding hands, whipping front and back, gliding all around the room. But that was the only time.

Grandma, Stevie, and I were still sitting in my room when Mom called us for dinner.

IT STARTED in the schoolyard during recess. Elaine and I were by the fence, when we heard yelling. A circle of kids had formed, but we couldn't see what was happening. All we heard was the yelling.

"Come on," Elaine said, pulling my sleeve. I didn't want to go over. Several rows of kids blocked our view, but she pushed in. When you're short, you can get away with that. I pulled my arm away and stayed in back.

"*Commie-pinko! Commie-pinko!*" The chant was picked up by the circle, but Charlie's voice was distinct. Elaine pushed back to stand next to me, her face flushed. "It's the Powser kid. Charlie's got him pinned down!"

I stared at her. "Why?"

"That paper, you know, the *Daily* something, it's on the ground next to him. Must've come out of his notebook. Charlie asked him if his father was a Commie. . . ."

My hands started to sweat. I've seen Brian Powser leaving Mrs. Manny's newsstand just as I've gotten there. It's out of the neighborhood for both of us. When we've passed each other, we've never said a word.

I could hear Charlie now. "Are you gonna tear it up, jerk, or do I have to?" Elaine jumped up and down to see over the kids' heads.

"Charlie's tearing it! He's tearing it!" she cried.

The circle started hollering, "*Rip it! Rip it! Rip it!*" Elaine was hollering too. I found myself saying the words, softly at first, *but saying them*. Me. And then louder, "*Rip it! Rip it!*"

"Leave him alone." Paul Shapiro elbowed his way inside the circle and stood facing Charlie. "Leave him alone, Charlie. What's wrong with you?" He pulled Charlie's arms off Brian. "He's got a paper, so what? Ever hear of free speech? This is free read. Back off."

The chanting stopped. Everybody waited for Charlie's response. You could see Charlie's brain figuring what he was going to do. Paul's bigger than him. Charlie leaned back and shoved his hands in his pockets.

"What's with you, Shapiro?" he snickered. "You defending Commie-pinkos now?" He grinned. "Which side are you on?"

Nobody uttered a sound. I wiped my hands on my skirt.

Gail Boseman shouted, "Hey, Paul, how about it? Which side you on?" The circle came alive again.

"Yeah, Paul! Which side you on?" The group wheeled on him like dive-bombing hawks.

"Leave him alone." Paul's voice was low but strong. He pushed his way back through the crowd. As he passed me, I turned away.

I don't know him! I screamed in my head. *I'm not connected to him.*

"I don't know," Elaine said. "He's cute, but . . ."

I felt sick. "See you later." I ran into the school. In the girls' room I splashed cold water on my face. Me, yelling, "Rip it!" How could those words come out of my mouth? I wish I could hide behind my hair like the Crazy Lady.

Someone was coming into the girls' room. I rushed into a stall and locked the door.

I made it through social studies and Mrs. Ridit, and math class after that. Then I went straight home.

Didn't even wait for Stevie. I just wanted to be out of there. I didn't see Elaine the next day except to wave in the hall. Usually we eat lunch together, but she had some assignment from the band teacher. And then it was the weekend.

I was by myself, hanging out on the stoop about eleven o'clock on Sunday. I still couldn't get over me yelling, "Rip it!" Elaine came by. "Hey, Jamie. Why don't you come with me? It's just me. My parents went to early Mass."

Elaine's Catholic, and goes to St. Helena's, which is near us. "Where do you go?" she'd asked me one time.

There are probably over a hundred apartment buildings here, divided into four quadrants. "Park Street Methodist on the North Side," I said. That was another lie. Mom's Jewish and Dad's Episcopalian, and nobody goes anywhere. The problem is, the whole world thinks you're weird if you don't go to church. Elaine never goes to the North Side, so she wouldn't know if there was a Methodist church over there.

It was a sunny day, and she squinted up at the bright sky. "Baby Jesus' head will be all lit up." She's talked a lot about baby Jesus and how great the stained-glass windows are. So why not? I ran upstairs to put on a skirt.

Inside Elaine's church there was a hum of whispers when we sat down in her pew. Could they tell I was half-Jewish, half-Episcopalian?

Elaine pointed to the right, high up. There was baby Jesus glowing in the sunlight. "It really is a beautiful window," I said. And I said that as a . . . what? Methodist? Jew? Episcopalian? Nothing?

Mom likes the Passover seder, and we have one, but she says it has nothing to do with religion. Uncle Maury also likes seders. "Chopped walnuts, apples, and wine. What's against it?"

They both say it's tradition, not God, they're celebrating. "It's the first great exodus for freedom." Mom says that every year.

And every year Grandma raises her glass. "A toast we should make to sweetening freedom with wine! *L'chayim!*"

"To life!" Mom and Uncle Maury say.

And Stevie and I shout, "Amen." That's as religious as we get. Dad doesn't even want a Christmas tree. "Trees belong with their roots in the earth," he says.

Dad and Uncle George don't agree about a lot of things, but I know they think the same thing about going to church. "If you want to pray," Dad once said, "you can do it at home without other people looking over your clothing."

Actually, I don't know what I think about religion. Uncle Maury says he's an atheist. From what Mom explained about agnostics, that's what I think I am. I mean, how can you know for sure if there's a God? Stevie is always asking if there's a heaven. He doesn't really like it when I tell him I have no idea.

"There's only a hell," Uncle Maury told us, "and it's for people who don't care about anything but their own pocketbooks."

HARRIET PURDUE'S name was still taped to the bottom shelf of my gym locker. Last year we shared the locker until her family moved away.

Elaine watched me tear the name tag off. "My father's keeping a count of how many Commies President Eisenhower says he's firing from government jobs. I think it's over a thousand."

"Harriet's father wasn't in the government. He taught college," I said.

"Same kind of thing. Besides, they're only getting what they deserve," she said. "I mean, they could take over everything." Her voice dribbled off. "Anyway, that's what my father says."

Me and Sherlock Holmes figured that was her father talking.

"I guess," I said.

Is that a lie? I'm not agreeing, so that's not a lie, but I'm not disagreeing, which is a lie. Everybody seems to think that all Communists are terrible people. Even Elaine.

"Why should Mr. Stingypuss Pennypincher the Third make so much money he can cool down on a hot summer day floating on a huge banana in a sea of ice cream, while the rest of us watch the dessert from the desert?"

"What?" Elaine stared at me like I was crazy.

"That's something my uncle used to say when Stevie and I were little kids."

Elaine shut her locker door. "I don't know what you're talking about."

"You know, why should some people have all the money and other people have a hard time getting enough food to eat?" I was thinking about Grandma's old newspaper clipping: "The people's cry for food reached the hearts of the soldiers."

Elaine looked at me like I was nuts. "Look," she said, "I'm just saying, let the president send the Commies back to Russia. Throw them out. Or you could, you know, like the Rosenbergs—"

She said their name! There was a buzz-saw sound in my ear. The noise got louder and louder. I could see Elaine's mouth moving, but I couldn't hear her. She had said their name. She must have said that other word. Electrocution! Killed by the government. Communist spies for Russia, the president said. I don't say their names, not to myself, not to anybody. It happened a couple of months ago. In my movie about me and this summer, every person will wear black. Never, ever, *ever* will I say those names out loud.

"What's the matter, Jamie? You look sick." Elaine was staring at me.

I shook my head. "I was thinking about Russia."

"Yeah, that does kind of make you sick." She closed her locker. "Do you think you'd know a Commie if you saw one?"

"I . . . I guess."

"Okay, girls. Positions!" The gym teacher ended that conversation, which was good because it could only get worse.

All I know about Russia is that workers got together and threw out the czar and made the new Soviet government. Uncle George says life is wonderful for ordinary people over there. Uncle Maury and Grandma say Stalin is a vicious dictator. That's as much as I want to know. Especially after this summer's electrocu—

When I got home from school, Barry banged on the pipe. That's when I remembered it's the day the Duncan yo-yo salesman waits on the corner. Thinking about you-know-what made me almost forget. I went down and met Barry on the stoop. For the record, I'm not the only one who lies. Barry does too, but about dumb things like yo-yos.

"I put on a new sleeper string last night," I said, "and I've been practicing rock-the-baby-in-the-cradle."

"Well, if you win today, it's 'cause of your new string." Barry always has some reason for losing. "Anyway, something's wrong with my string," he said.

I hit a crack, and my yo-yo wobbled and scraped on the sidewalk. "How you going to do cradle when you can't even walk the dog?" He laughed as he dogged around me.

"Hey, big shot." I whipped past him and turned around. "Spanning the world," I said, imitating the movie newsreel man, as my yo-yo made a neat circle in the air.

He glared at me and spun his yo-yo, but it shot out at an angle when it's supposed to be straight.

"You're twisting your hand just before you throw."

"It's the wind," he said.

P.S. My cradle was so good, the yo-yo man gave me a Duncan insignia ring. Barry grumbled all the way home.

✦　✦　✦

Aunt Sheila was in our apartment, and without Uncle George, which told me something was up.

"What?" Mom said, leaning forward in her chair. Aunt Sheila whispers, even when we're in the house.

"Oh, Rachel, it was awful. Mollie Fishbein was called in by the principal." Aunt Sheila twisted a tissue. "She has to go before the Board of Ed and answer questions or pack up her desk."

Aunt Sheila and Mollie Fishbein teach together at P.S. 115 on the North Side. When Dad got home, Mom and Aunt Sheila were still talking about Mrs. Fishbein.

"I know she won't answer their questions," Aunt Sheila said.

"It's a matter of principle, and from what I know about Mollie," Dad said, "I can't imagine her talking to the board."

"She came to Hazel Delaney's retirement party. They were taking lots of pictures," Aunt Sheila said, "but she's not . . . " her voice lowered to a whisper " . . . in the party."

There is definitely something weird about whispering in your own relatives' house.

"Guilt by association," Mom said. "Mollie raises a glass with friends, and suddenly she's guilty because of their politics. Besides, Mollie doesn't know anything, so she couldn't talk even if she wanted to."

"But if she did know something, what would she be guilty of?" Dad said. "She hasn't done anything against the law. It isn't a crime to want economic and social equality for people. And it isn't against the law to be in the Communist Party."

Mrs. Ridit had been really hammering about this stuff, so I said, "In social studies class, Mrs. Ridit says the Communists are trying to take over the world, and now Russia has the atom bomb. She says Alger Hiss who worked in our own government was convicted of spying for Russia." They all looked at me like I'd brought a raging bull into the living room.

"Hiss has always denied being a Communist or a spy," Dad said. "And he was convicted of lying, not spying."

"But what about the other stuff?"

Aunt Sheila kept twisting that tissue.

"Listen, Jamie," Dad continued, "fundamentally, Communism is about changing an economic system so that there are no terrible social inequities."

"But Mrs. Ridit keeps saying the Communist Party believes in overthrowing the government."

As I said that, I realized for all the talk about politics in our house, and these days there was more than I could stand, Mom and Dad have never actually said anything about the Communist Party. Dad doesn't even talk much about the Soviet Union. He says we have to worry about making America better.

"'Violent overthrow,' these red-baiters talk about," Mom said. "I don't know anyone stockpiling guns or bombs to overthrow the government, or even thinking about it. But the fastest way to stop debate about racial equality, or paying workers a decent wage, or getting housing for the homeless, is to yell 'Communist!' Then everyone shuts up."

Aunt Sheila couldn't sit still. "Poor Mollie."

"The point is," Dad said, "we don't live in the Soviet Union. These school boards and committees of Congress tell us all the time how lucky we are to live in America, where we can say whatever we want. They tell us how different this is from life under a Communist dictatorship, and then they tell us what we are allowed to think and say." Dad looked grim.

My head was spinning. I left and went to practice rock-the-cradle. I wonder if whoever went after Mollie Fishbein will go to South Side High, where Dad teaches senior math.

"BRING THAT up here this minute!" Mrs. Ridit point-ed to the picture in my hand. Elaine had sent away for two 8 x 10 glossy photos, and she had just passed me one. Her allowance is bigger than mine. She's very generous that way.

"This instant!" Mrs. Ridit repeated.

Everybody stared at me as I walked up to the front desk.

"Face the class and hold it up," she said. "What is that, Miss Morse?"

Everybody could see what it was. "It's Gregory Peck," I said. Mrs. Ridit glared at me. "Ma'am," I added.

"And where did you get it?"

My heart stopped for a minute. "I don't know, ma'am." I absolutely wasn't going to say Elaine passed it to me.

"*You . . . don't . . . know?*" Mrs. Ridit drew out each word. The girls in the front row giggled.

"I found it," I said in an almost-whisper.

She turned to the class. "Is there anybody who knows how Jamie Morse got this?"

Not a sound.

She turned back to me. "We have been discussing the spread of Communism around the world . . . unless of course you haven't been listening."

She glared at me. I nodded.

"Well then, you will write a report on Communists in Hollywood, and turn it in on Monday. And . . ." She paused. "I expect you to *write* it, not *find* it." The giggles were now unrestrained.

Gregory Peck, torn in half, dropped into the trash can. Elaine stared down at her notebook as I passed her desk.

"I'm really sorry," she said in the hall.

"It's all right."

"Thanks. I mean, if she'd turned around a minute before, she'd have seen me passing you the picture."

We walked to our lockers to get our lunch bags, and headed for the cafeteria. "You're really brave, Jamie, you know that?"

I stared at her. Brave? I'm scared to death. "That's me," I joked, "like John Wayne."

"I really mean it, jerko. You know what? I'll help you find stuff for Mrs. Ridit."

"I'm not *finding* anything this time," I said. We both laughed.

"I could ask my father about Commies and Hollywood. He knows things," Elaine said.

"I think Mrs. Ridit is going to want me to list where I got stuff, and I'm not going to write down 'Elaine's father.'"

"I was only trying to help."

"Come on." I poked her. "Let's have a lunch without Mrs. Ridit's face looking up at me from a glass of milk. She doesn't go with peanut butter and jelly. You know what I mean?"

But it wasn't Mrs. Ridit I thought about at lunch. It was movies. I really don't want to know about Communism and Hollywood. Movies are movies, and that's all I want them to be.

"Remember those people they called the 'Hollywood Ten'?" Elaine said. "It was when my father was checking out who was in every movie I saw."

"Yeah, a couple of years ago," I said.

You bet I remembered. It was the first time I had heard that people were sent to jail because somebody said they were Communists.

"Dammit," Dad had said. "All everybody's worried about is these damn movie people who may have to give up their swimming pools. How about the Baltimore steelworkers who were fired? They lost a lot more than a swimming pool."

Mom didn't say anything.

"Come on, Rachel," he said, "admit it. It's a little tougher on a hundred-dollar-a-week man than on a thousand-dollar one."

Mom stared at him. "Leave it to a math teacher to think only about numbers. What about public humiliation? Doesn't that count, Mr. Numbers? Larry Parks's movie career died. He's as much out of a job as a steelworker."

"A perfect example of the absurdity of it all," Dad said. "Larry Parks who—for what, six months?—belonged to the Communist Party, and he even gives the committee names of people he saw at meetings. So they too can lose their jobs. In the end it doesn't matter. He's still done for."

"So you do care about the 'swimming pool set,'" Mom said.

Dad shrugged. "It's only going to get worse," he predicted. Mom said that was the one thing they agreed on.

I must have looked sick, because Grandma took me into the bedroom.

"Your mama and papa aren't famous. Nothing will happen to them," she said softly. And then I knew why I was upset. All this was before last summer and the Rosenb—I feel like running to Grandma now and shouting, *Nobody knew who they were, and look what happened to them!*

Elaine looked at me like she'd said something, and where was I.

"Yeah," I said. "I remember the Hollywood Ten."

"Look up your subject in the *Reader's Guide to Periodical Literature*," Mrs. Finley said. She's been the head of the public library ever since I've had a library card, which is way back when Mom taught me how to write my name. I can never figure out if Mrs. Finley's got a cold, or if she's snorting in irritation into the handkerchief she always pulls out. She pointed to the reference shelves, and turned back to her work.

By the time Elaine arrived I'd written down all the issues of *Time* magazine that had articles about the Hollywood Ten and the House Un-American Activities Committee. Mrs. Ridit likes *Time* magazine.

We both sat reading. "Isn't it weird," Elaine said, "how the committee members call these witnesses the 'unfriendlies' because they wouldn't tell the committee if they're Communist or not. I mean, if they're Commies, they're a lot worse than 'unfriendly,' don't you think?"

"Yeah," I said. Lie number 723 today. "And listen to this. *For Whom the Bell Tolls*, did you ever see that?" Elaine shook her head. "Me neither. Anyway, the director told the committee, 'These Communists thump their chests and call themselves liberals, but if you drop their rompers you'll find a hammer and sickle on their rear ends.' And that's a quote!"

We both burst into laughter. "Rompers!" Elaine said. "I never heard underpants called that before."

"Maybe I should put that in my report," I said. But the next part wasn't funny. "Jack Warner, the head of Warner Brothers studio refused to hire some writers because he suspected them."

"So?" Elaine said.

I picked at the paint on my pencil. "What if he wanted to fire someone, but he didn't have a good reason? So he says he 'suspects' the guy."

"Come on, Jamie. It's real serious to say somebody's a Commie. Nobody'd make that up."

"Yeah? Well, some of this is nutty. You know Adolphe Menjou?" I said. "The little guy with the twirly mustache. He was in *Across the Wide Missouri*." Elaine nodded. "Well," I said, "he's a 'friendly.'" I pointed to the page. "He says, quote, 'Anyone attending any meeting at which Paul Robeson appears, and applauds, can be considered a Communist.' Can you believe that—applauds!"

"Who's Paul Robeson?"

"He's this singer."

Elaine chewed on her lower lip. "Well, maybe he *is* a Communist. I don't know."

"Maybe you clap because you love his singing," I said.

We have some Paul Robeson records, which of course I didn't say. And I love his singing. His voice is so deep and soft, it wraps around you like one of Grandma's feather pillows.

She shrugged, and we both went back to reading.

Paul Robeson's face fills the screen. The camera pulls back. He's on stage at a huge outdoor concert. The camera turns. Dad and Mom are sitting there smiling, clapping. Cops come from each side of the screen. They grab first Mom, then Dad, and handcuff them. The screen turns black.

"Who's Ring Lardner Jr.?" Elaine said. "It says here he's one of the Hollywood Ten."

"Yeah. I'm reading about him right now. A movie writer."

"Did he write something bad?"

"I can't tell. This article just says that when the committee chairman asked him, 'Are you now or have you ever been a Communist?' he said, 'I could answer you the way you want—'"

"'—but I won't because I'd hate myself in the morning.'" Mrs. Finley finished the sentence.

"I don't understand," Elaine said.

Mrs. Finley tapped her pencil eraser on the page I had been reading from. "Mr. Lardner is saying that nobody has the right to question him about his political beliefs."

"So if he answered the committee," I said, "he'd betray his principles?"

"The First Amendment," Mrs. Finley said. "You have the right to your beliefs, and no law can abridge your freedom of speech." She took off her glasses. "Ten minutes until closing, girls. And please return the books to the shelf." She was back to her sharp voice.

"Maybe she's like that 'cause her rompers are too tight," Elaine said. "That's it! You should call your paper, 'The Ridit Romper Report' by Jamie Morse."

We both giggled. But I know I didn't think it was as funny as Elaine did.

MRS. RIDIT didn't say a word when I handed in my report. I left out the rompers. I left out a lot of stuff, but I did write down what Ring Lardner Jr. said. I had to after Mrs. Finley explained it. I don't know what Mrs. Ridit will think. She's pretty ignorant. "Nucular war," she says, cross my heart.

We're doing a geography project, and the trouble started near the end of the period. Mrs. Ridit has us divided into continent groups, with each person in a group making a report on a particular country. She's never asked us for suggestions, so I don't know why she did today. I bet she never does again.

"Now, class, how might we coordinate the different research groups?" Silence. "Yes? Any ideas?"

Lily D'Amato raised her hand. "We could have a classroom United Nations." It was as if Lily had dropped a "nucular" bomb. Any minute I expected the air-raid bell to go off, and we'd be lined up in the hall, facing the wall with our arms over our heads. Poor Lily. She didn't have Mrs. Ridit last year, so I guess she doesn't know. The United Nations! Mrs. Ridit's eyebrows met her hairline. Nobody said a word. Not even Charlie. We all waited for her to speak.

"Supporters of the United Nations say their goal is one government for all countries," she said at last. "And these one-worlders are most likely what we would call 'fellow travelers.'" Fellow travelers, she explained, are not actual members of the Communist Party, but they might as well be, since they go along with what the Communists say. "They travel side by side, hence, fellow travelers," she said, as if it were the cleverest thing in the world.

"Actually, Mrs. Ridit . . ."

Paul. I can't imagine anyone else interrupting Mrs. Ridit.

". . . isn't the U.N. a place where countries meet to talk and not shoot at each other?"

I pressed my lips together till they hurt. The room was still.

"Pinko talk!" Charlie said in a loud whisper. Mrs.

Ridit reminded him to raise his hand before speaking, but she smiled.

I made it through Mrs. Ridit and met Elaine in the schoolyard after the last class. "Sandy can't come over," she said. "But you're still coming, right?" I nodded.

I was looking forward to new movie magazines, but wouldn't you know it, Mr. Reilly was home. He looked up from his newspaper when Elaine and I walked in, and motioned for us to sit down. Elaine glanced at me and nodded toward the couch.

"So," Mr. Reilly said. "What have they been teaching you girls?" He jabbed his finger at something in the newspaper. "I hope they're telling you what's going on in the world?" He didn't sound hopeful. He sounded angry.

"Like what?" Elaine asked. Boy, was that the worst thing to say.

Mr. Reilly put down the paper. "The country's not safe, nobody's safe," he said, "and we won't be until we root out all the Russia-loving radicals." Mr. Reilly rolled up his newspaper and began smacking it on his leg like a nightstick. "Reds—they want to end private property. Can you imagine that! Force their system on us, and overthrow everything we live by." He snapped open the paper and began to read.

Elaine headed for her room, and I followed. She pulled out her three-ring binder. "Trade you a Gregory Peck for your Farley Granger," she said. She so loved Farley Granger, I knew I could get two for one.

"If you throw in the one where he's got his hands on his hips."

"Nope. But you can have an Ava Gardner." Elaine had a huge collection of Ava Gardner. She was such a fan, the studio sent her doubles after she organized a fan club. I'm not crazy about Ava Gardner. Besides, I was having a hard time paying attention. I kept hearing that whack as Mr. Reilly struck his leg.

Suddenly I wanted to go home. "Okay," I said. "Deal."

Mr. Reilly's kind of scary. Dad is definitely not scary. When I got home, he was in his chair reading, and Mom was in the kitchen. Uncle George and Aunt Sheila were over for dessert. It's hard to picture Dad and his brothers all in the same family. Dad's quiet, Uncle George is loud, and Uncle Joe, well, he's probably the bravest person I ever heard about.

Grandma brought the coffeepot into the living room. I can always tell when Uncle George is about to make a speech, and boy, was I right.

"By God, Petey, nobody had to teach us to side with the downtrodden, because we were the downtrodden."

He poked Dad, who always looks uncomfortable when Uncle George calls him Petey and talks about their childhood.

"Not again, George," Mom said impatiently. "We know the story."

When Dad was four, Uncle George six, and Uncle Joe eight, their mother died, and the boys were sent to a county orphanage in Nebraska. Mom, not Dad, told us about it. The brothers only saw their father one time after that, when he came to tell them he was going West to start over. He promised to send for them, but they never heard from him again. That's my grandfather nobody talks about.

"Yessiree, we were forged in that orphanage."

Stevie and I looked at each other. Uncle George always tries to make himself the center of every conversation. He leaned back. "But there are no suffering orphan children in the Soviet Union."

"So the government comes and kisses everyone good night?" Grandma could look at you and knit without ever dropping a stitch.

Stevie giggled. "And no one to make you wash behind your ears."

"Nothing glamorous about being an orphan," Dad said. "Here or in Russia. The world doesn't like to look at what's not pretty."

"But," Uncle George said with a smile, "under

Communism, the government provides everything, even more than most families can give." He stretched his legs, settling in for a long listen to his own voice. "Our system is rotten to the core, Petey boy. But when you transfer the means of production—"

This time Grandma put down her knitting. "Don't forget the people, George." Grandma's the only one who can stop him. "Not fancy words—system schmystem!" And she waved her hand. "That's that."

The more excited Grandma gets, the more she makes up English, but you always know what she means. She picked up her knitting and began to hum. I peeked at Uncle George. He looked confused. Everybody started talking about something else, not politics.

I went into the kitchen, and when I came back I heard Mom say, "I think Mr. Nathan uses his belt on Charlie. Maury heard whacking and what sounded like crying."

Charlie? Crying?

"ANY VOLUNTEERS for this past summer's current events roundup?" Iris Fleming asked. She and Nate Winters are the *NB* coeditors-in-chief. I sat so still anyone taking a pulse would have pronounced me dead. Timmy Murphy got the assignment. I volunteered to report on the preparations for the Halloween costume party. Okay, Dad, you were right.

"If I'm covering the Rosenberg execution," Timmy said, "maybe we could have a box with the headline 'DEAD REDS.' Better dead Reds than live ones!" Everybody laughed. Except me.

Mr. Tubell scraped his chair as he stood up and walked from the back of the room to his desk. "The Rosenbergs were accused of spying, isn't that right? And they were Communists."

Everybody nodded.

"Are all Communists in America spies?"

"I don't get it," Timmy said. "We're talking about American atomic spies who gave secrets to Russia. It's good they're dead."

Mr. Tubell nodded. "Spying against your country is wrong. But put the Rosenbergs to one side for the moment. I'm asking something else. Do you think every American Communist is a spy?"

"How do we know?" Nate said.

"Well, what do you think Communists believe in?"

There was a lot of shuffling in seats.

"They're against us," Joey said.

"But what are they *for*? Come on, people," Mr. Tubell said. "Don't think about Russia. Think about an American who says he's a Communist. What does he want?"

"Economic justice?"

That was me!

"And what does that mean?"

Everybody stared at me. My hands were totally clammy. Economic justice was a phrase I'd heard a lot in our house. Fragments, words from the dinner table popped into my head—"No super rich or very poor people. It's not fair that the people who work the hardest earn only a little, and the bosses take home most of the money."

"So Communists care about fairness," Mr. Tubell said. "What else?"

"They stir up trouble about Negroes," Timmy said.

I thought of those rallies I'd been at with Dad and Mom, trying to get the Harpers an apartment.

Mr. Tubell leaned against the blackboard. "Are you saying, Timmy, that if Communists are for something, you're against it?"

"You bet."

"So if Communists are against racial prejudice, you are for it?"

Timmy started to say something, then stopped. A lot of kids were smiling. "That was a good one," Nate whispered to Joey.

Mr. Tubell went on. "Let's say you're a Communist, and you believe in economic equality. Does that make you a spy?"

We all sat very still.

"Maybe you don't agree with the Communists, but do they have a right to their opinions?"

"But," Timmy insisted, "their opinions are really bad."

"Okay," said Mr. Tubell. "So what do you do in a

democratic country when you don't agree with someone's opinions?"

"You vote against them," I said. I felt like Grandma
was sitting next to me.

"My dad's in a union," Iris said. "Not a Communist
one," she said quickly. "He's against the Communists,
but," she nodded toward me, "he also says the bosses
make too much money."

"So people you disagree with can have some good
ideas?" Mr. Tubell wrote the word UNION in capital
letters on the board. He drew a line under it and said,
"Picture this. You're in a union. What do you want?"

"Little work, lots of money," someone said.

"Shorter work week & pay increase," Mr. Tubell
wrote. He turned to us. "Now that's a good idea."

Everybody laughed, even me.

"Extra pay for overtime," someone else said.

"Money if you get sick."

"Vacation time."

Mr. Tubell wrote it all down. "So unions want better working conditions."

"Not Commie unions. They want to take over, just
like they want to take over the government," Timmy
said.

"Come on, Timmy, what's with you?" Iris said.
"You're not a Commie just because you want a fair
salary." She sounded mad.

"I don't know," Nate said. "It's not just about working conditions. They hate religion in Russia, and my father says they're atheistic."

"Don't you have a right *not* to believe in God?" I asked.

Nate was silent for a minute. "I guess," he said. "But they shouldn't force you *not* to believe."

Joey raised his hand. "My grandmother says, back in Italy lots of people are in the Communist Party, but lots of them still go to church."

"So," Mr. Tubell said, "Communist parties can be different in different countries. Is that what you're saying?"

Joey chewed a fingernail. "I suppose."

"And what about Americans? Do all of us support everything our government says and does?"

Nate grinned. "Republicans and Democrats fight all the time."

"They certainly do. So do you think all American Communists support everything the Soviet Union does?"

Timmy exploded. "This is crazy. A Communist is a Communist, wherever he is. And my father says their whole system is rotten. People aren't equal. There will always be rich and poor." He paused and laughed. "You just gotta be on the rich side."

You know how they say, "It was so quiet, you

could hear a pin drop"? Well, you could.

"Can you think of anything 'rotten,' to use your word, Timmy, that's happened here in America?" Mr. Tubell looked at us and waited.

"Slavery," Iris said.

"President Harding and the Teapot Dome Scandal," said Joey. "We just studied that."

Mr. Tubell sat at his desk, leaning back with his hands behind his head. Kids kept on talking, asking questions, answering them, disagreeing. Me? I didn't say another word.

After a while Iris and Nate went back to NB business. By the time the bell rang, we all had our assignments. In the hall Nate and Timmy were talking. "Those creeps deserved to be killed," Timmy said. "They were spies against us. Against their own country."

The Rosenbergs. Hard to believe it was just a couple of months ago. Mid-June, a Friday night, almost eight o'clock, and they were all in the living room by the radio. Mom, Dad, Uncle Maury, Aunt Sheila, Uncle George, and Grandma. Waiting. Ice statues, frozen in place. Even Stevie. Nine years old, and he too sat waiting for Julius and Ethel Rosenberg to die. Everyone on the planet was probably listening, and all I wanted was to push my fingers deep into my ears to shut it all out.

"See you later," I said. I sounded like a dying frog. Dad blinked.

"Where you going, Jamie? Can I come?"

"Sit still, Stevie," Mom said.

The Rosebergs weren't guilty. That's one thing everybody in my family agreed on. The grown-ups all hoped there'd be a pardon. Maybe President Eisenhower would change his mind at the last minute and let them live. But I knew it wouldn't happen. The government wanted them to die. The judge in the trial said because of their spying, thousands of Americans were dying in the Korean War. It didn't seem to matter to the president that millions of people marched in protest against the execution. It didn't matter how many rallies there had been all over the world. It didn't matter that even the pope had called for mercy. They were going to die.

When I got back, Dad was alone in the living room, staring at the silent radio. His cigarette ash was long and about to fall. I looked at him. I wasn't angry anymore. I wanted him to talk to me, say something, tell me how this could happen.

He sat not moving, and I turned away. Stevie's light was off, but his door was open. I could just make him out, sitting at the far corner of his bed in a cannonball position. He was wiping his eyes, like he didn't want me to see he was crying.

"Jamie?"

"Yeah."

"Where'd you go?"

"Just out." He waited for me to say more. I sat on his bed.

His voice sounded like it came from five miles down inside him. "Do you think they'll fry Daddy?"

I flinched. Kids had all said "fry" before the execution. It was so unreal. But now they were dead. It had an awful sound.

"Naw, they won't. He's not Jewish."

Stevie was quiet. "Okay," he said. "Not Uncle George either 'cause he's Daddy's brother. But what about Uncle Maury?"

I thought about that. "Nope. He's a Socialist. They're after Communists."

Stevie seemed satisfied. Suddenly he grabbed my arm. "But Mommy. She's married to Dad and she's Jewish!"

That took me longer. "Mom's not famous," I said at last, "so they don't care about her."

He thought for a minute, then nodded. He uncurled completely and stretched out on his back. "'Night, Jamie." He rolled over and faced the wall.

The day after the execution, Mom packed up several cartons of books. I didn't look at them, but I knew they were about politics. "We need the room," she said. I'd never seen her get rid of books before. She and Dad buy books all the time. And what they don't buy, we take out of the library.

Mom looked like she'd been up all night. "Uncle Maury will bring the truck later and pick them up," was all she said.

Uncle Maury drives a truck for Samson Brothers' Very Fresh Vegetables & Fruits, Inc. When he buys a box of Florida grapefruits during the winter, he brings it home on the subway. He doesn't use the truck for personal jobs. Never. He's very particular about that. Now Mom was getting rid of books, and Uncle Maury was packing the cartons in his truck.

Mom's bric-a-brac collection of miniature porcelain birds replaced the books.

MR. TUBELL'S gone, and nobody's telling us anything. Twenty-two years, and a Mr. Bracton is sitting at Mr. Tubell's desk. MR. BRACTON is printed on the blackboard. Bric-a-Bracton, I keep thinking.

During recess, the *NB* staff hung out together. Charlie came over. "Cleaning house, huh, guys?" He grinned.

"What do you mean?" Iris asked.

"Pinkos, simple as that."

"You don't know what you're talking about," Iris snapped. "Mr. Tubell's great."

Charlie looked at Nate. "Don't you talk to your coeditor? I told you after all that Rosenberg stuff, my dad said the school board was meeting about ole Mr. T."

Nate looked embarrassed.

"Maybe he's just out sick," I blurted out.

Charlie snorted. "Got what he deserved."

I don't care if Mr. Nathan beats Charlie. All Mr. Tubell did was start a class discussion.

"Figures," Timmy said in a half whisper to Nate. "You don't talk about those spy finks like that." Nate looked away.

Stevie and I walked home from school. Barry was waiting for me on the stoop. "I got an Appaloosa," he said. "And you gotta see it now, 'cause I'm not feeling so good."

"Be down in a couple of minutes." I'd been looking for an Appaloosa for my trading card collection, but when I dropped off my books, I was too upset about Mr. Tubell to do any trading. I went back down. "I've got to pick up something for my mom," I said. "I'll look tomorrow morning before school, okay?"

"I don't know, maybe. Depends how I feel."

"You look green," Stevie said. Barry went upstairs. Stevie looked at me. "Well, he did."

I walked and walked, staring at the sidewalk.

When I looked up I'd gone all the way over into the North Side. I crossed Metro Avenue and headed toward the candy store on the corner. I needed a Mounds bar bad.

"Hey, Jamie."

I looked over at the soda fountain. "Harriet. Hi."

"What are you doing over here?"

"Nothing really. Just walking."

"Well, see you."

Probably not, but I nodded. Harriet's gone. Mr. Tubell's gone. Who's next?

After dinner I told everyone that Mr. Tubell was replaced by a Mr. Bracton. Mom turned pale. Grandma got up and took the dishes into the kitchen.

"It's not going to happen, Rachel," Dad said. "I'm a math teacher, and a good one. You've seen the annual reviews—'Excellent,' they all say. Don't worry, it's not going to happen."

"How can you say that? Mark Twain has 'excellent reviews,' and they've whipped his books out of the public library."

"Yeah," I said. "They didn't have *A Connecticut Yankee in King Arthur's Court*. And when I asked Mrs. Finley, all she said was, 'It's a terrible shame.'" Mom looked at me. "Really, Mom, that's all she said."

"Look," Dad continued, "McCarthy is using his

committee to smear anybody he can get his hands on. He's looking for headlines, and Mark Twain is famous." Dad turned to me. "Right, Jamie? Listen, Rachel, I'm not famous—except maybe in your eyes—"

"This isn't funny," Mom said.

Dad held out his hands. "I don't have any books on library shelves. McCarthy's not coming after me."

"You don't get it, do you, Pete? If they can go after Mark Twain, they can go after anybody. Like Tubell. Like us."

Mom sounded really scared. I was breathing quickly.

"Mr. T. is gone . . . he's gone . . . Mr. T. is gone" went round and round in my head, like a little kid's skipping rhyme. I felt cold.

The smear on the middle of the page looked like a bloodstain. Mr. Tubell was crushed flat, his life juices squeezed out of him, right in the middle of the *T* volume of the *Encyclopedia Britannica*. Dead as a pressed flower.

I knew it was a nightmare as I was dreaming it, but I couldn't stop. In the dream, Mr. Tubell's black mustache tilted in toward the binding of the book, like a broken leaf. The *NB* staff held hands in a circle around the desk. Timmy shouted, "Off with his head!" I pushed him out of the circle. Iris called for a proper burial, and I started to remove Mr. Tubell from the page.

The telephone ring jarred me awake and pushed away the dream. I heard low voices. Then louder. I opened my door.

"Pete, wait!" Mom stood in the doorway of their bedroom. Stevie was in the hall. Dad brushed past him, already dressed.

"Pete, your shoes!"

Dad was still in his slippers. "The hell with it," he said, and went out the front door.

Mom went into the living room, clutching her arms across her chest. Grandma came out of her room fully dressed. "Get your clothes on," she said to me and Stevie.

Mom sat in the throne chair. It swallowed her up. Dad came back with a couple of newspapers. He stood over the dining room table reading the front page of the *New York Times*. His face was gray. After a few minutes he said, "I suppose it's a good thing Maury is up so early and called. We know what's coming." Nobody said a word. The only sound was the rustle of the newspaper. "Mollie. Poor Mollie," Dad said. He went to make a pot of coffee, and I looked at the front page.

RED TEACHERS EXPOSED
BOARD SPOKESMAN SAYS

According to the reporter, an anonymous informer had testified before the Board of Education that "Peter Morse and Mollie Fishbein are members of the Communist Party. Mr. Morse, age forty-one, teaches tenth-, eleventh-, and twelfth-grade mathematics at South Side High School. Although he's been at the school for nearly twenty years, a Board of Education spokesman said, 'There is no seniority or leniency when it comes to subversives.'"

I didn't read about Mollie Fishbein.

Mom stood up. "I'm going into the shower. When the coffee's ready, bring me a cup, Jamie. And take the paper into the bedroom."

Stevie had the paper on the rug. He was hunched over it, reading and biting his fingernails. I'd never seen him do that. I pulled his hand out of his mouth. "Leave me alone," he cried, and ran into the kitchen.

Grandma sat straight up in her rocking chair, hands folded in her lap, eyes clear, as if they could see across oceans. "Be ready," was all she said.

READY OR not, here we come. Stevie held his books pressed to his chest. We walked to school not saying a word. Barry didn't meet us on the stoop, even though I banged the pipe to let him know when we were leaving.

"I bet he's not talking to us," I said.

Stevie looked up at me. "Don't you remember? He said he was sick. I told you he looked green."

"I guess."

Every couple of minutes Stevie glanced up at me, but I stayed focused on the sidewalk. I knew he was scared, but so was I. As we crossed into the school-yard, I said, "I'll try to get out early at recess to catch you before you go in." He nodded. The cowlick at the back of his head bobbed, like it was on alert. Stevie could never keep it down, even with spitting on his hand and patting it all day long. I wished he was patting it now. Instead, he was biting the side of his finger. He looked very small as he climbed the stairs to go to his classroom.

In my homeroom, five of the *NB* staff were standing around Timmy's desk. They looked up when I came in. No one said a word. I walked to my seat and put my books down. The group broke up. I went over to hand Nate my article.

Another kid came up. "Hey, Nate. Do you think I should interview a couple of teachers for my piece?" Nate began an involved discussion. I left my story on top of his notebook. Kids were talking, but nobody said anything to me.

Mr. Bracton came in with a sheaf of papers and glanced briefly at me. Did his lips tighten? Does he read the paper before eight o'clock in the morning? Do the kids know?

The bell rang, and the room crackled with the sound of the assistant principal announcing the schedule for the day. We stood for the pledge of allegiance. ". . . one nation, indivisible, with liberty and justice for all."

Mr. Bracton distributed the new assignment sheets, and then the second bell released us into the hall.

"Jamie, wait up!" It was a relief to hear Elaine's voice. I had been hugging my books so tightly, I had a cramp in my side. "My mother gave me a couple of nut cookies for you." She smiled as she rushed off. "See you at lunch in the caf." Elaine's still talking to me.

Classes were endless. I didn't raise my hand, and no one called on me. At 11:45 I headed for the cafeteria.

"Hi, Jamie." It was the new girl in English class. Another person who didn't know.

I had brought a peanut butter and jelly sandwich from home, and stood on line to get a glass of milk. The food servers were as busy as ever. They snap at you if you don't move along fast enough. Elaine came up with a nickname for them—the hair nettles, in honor of the hairnets they have to wear. In some story she'd read, the villain got a mysterious rash from brushing against a patch of prickly nettles. That's how the hero identified the villain. We thought it was perfect for the prickly cafeteria ladies.

Today they looked more tired to me than cranky. Two of the three ladies had gray hair. How come I'd never noticed that? How old were they, anyway? Didn't you retire when you got to be that old?

I didn't see Elaine at any of the tables. Maybe she got stuck with blackboard duty. I sat by myself at a corner table. Maybe everyone knew, I don't know. Maybe they'd talk to me. Maybe they wouldn't. Maybe they'd never talk to me again. I shoved the rest of my sandwich back into the bag, and headed out to the schoolyard. I stayed there until the next class bell.

When school let out, I looked for Stevie, but not for long. I wanted to be anyplace but there.

"Be ready," Grandma had said. I kept looking behind me as I walked home. *Maybe the Purdy Street gang will get me.* I haven't thought about them in a long time. Nobody I know has ever seen them, but everybody knows what they do. If they catch you, they torture you with lit matches under your fingernails. I don't even know where Purdy Street is.

I made it to Baumgarten's Bakery. Mom had given me money to pick up a rye bread on my way home. I usually ask Mrs. Baumgarten, "What's that delicious perfume?" She's always covered in a light coating of white dust, a mix of flour and sugar. It's one of our jokes. Not today. I couldn't smell anything. I ordered without looking at her. "Rye bread, sliced with seeds."

I kept my head down. Every time I'm there she asks, "So how's your mama, and your fine papa?" Her son had Dad for math in high school, and now he's studying accounting at City College. Dad's a saint to them. Please let her not say anything. I've given up guessing what people will do. Maybe she won't sell me a loaf of rye.

"How's your mama, and your fine papa?" Mrs. Baumgarten said. When I looked up, she wasn't smiling.

"Your *fine* papa," she repeated.

"Don't you worry," she said fiercely as she pushed hard on the slicing machine. When I got home, I discovered she'd put five cookies in the bread bag. Mrs. Baumgarten will be a star in one of my movies, for sure.

Stevie was in the apartment when I got home. Neither of us wanted to talk much. Dinner was meat loaf. Stevie did not ask for more, which was unusual. Mom hardly talked, also unusual, and weirdest of all was what Dad said.

"It was Henry Taylor. He gave them my name."

"He's the moneymouse informer?" Stevie asked.

"Anonymous informer," Dad said. "Somebody whose name you don't know. But I found out. Henry Taylor."

"Good god, Pete, he's . . . he's been here . . . he's a friend. . . ." Mom covered her mouth.

"A friend, you say? An un-friend, is righter!" Grandma's hair was flopping down the sides of her face as she scratched at it.

"Mr. Taylor? The man you play cards with?" I said. Dad nodded.

"Dirty rat!" Stevie said.

Dad looked at him and me. "Mr. Henry Taylor is a sad and pathetic man, and you have to feel sorry for someone like that."

"Feel sorry for him?" I was almost shouting. "The Crazy Lady is sad and pathetic. Not Mr. Dirty Rat Taylor!"

You should have heard Uncle Maury. Dad tried to calm him, but that only made Mom mad. She turned on Dad. "He's your brother-in-law, for heaven's sake! He's part of this family. He has a right to be furious. How can you be so calm?" She scraped her chair back. "I'm making coffee. You can pour your own when it's ready."

The camera widens to show a family—parents and kids, uncles and aunts—trying to cover themselves as they stand on a subway platform, naked.

Crashing sounds came from the kitchen, and the water seemed to gush out of the faucet with a fury that matched Mom's. "You don't have to murder the pot," Uncle Maury said.

Then the doorbell rang.

"I DON'T believe it." Uncle Maury stood with his hands balled into fists. It was Mr. Henry Taylor. Uncle Maury stepped forward, and Mr. Rat Fink Taylor flinched. He looked past Uncle Maury to Dad. "Pete, let me explain."

Mom stood in the kitchen doorway. "I don't think it's a good idea for you to be here," she said. Her voice was ice.

"Please, Pete, let me come in. Let me explain," Mr. Taylor begged.

Dad stood up and nodded almost imperceptibly.

Uncle Maury didn't move, and Mr. Taylor had to squeeze around him.

Dad sat down in the big chair, his hands resting on his knees. Nobody said a word. Stevie stood rigid next to me.

"Stevie, bring Mr. Taylor a glass of water." Grandma was the first to break the silence. I'd been staring at Dad. Now I looked at Mr. Taylor. No wonder Grandma sent for water. He was licking his lips and rolling his eyes like he was going to pass out. His hands fluttered at his side. Mr. Taylor, the rat, looked like a baby bird that had fallen out of the nest.

"Yes?" was all Dad said.

The word was like a key that turns on an engine. "My God, Pete," Mr. Taylor said, "they gave me no choice."

Dad's eyebrows rose.

"No, I mean it. What could I do? If I didn't talk to them, I'd be out of a job. And once they've got you in that committee room, the only thing they really want is other names." He rubbed his hands as if trying to warm them. "The terrible truth is, they already know the names. They're not after information. They're showing you who's boss and getting pleasure out of making you grovel."

"Not everybody grovels, you bastard," Uncle Maury said in a menacing voice. He stood looking down at Mr. Taylor, who was sitting on the couch.

"Let him talk, Maury," Dad said. "Let him say what he came to say."

Mr. Taylor's eyes darted back and forth from Dad to Uncle Maury and back to Dad. He looked even more like a bird, with his skinny neck twisting first this way, then that. "Listen, Pete, when your name came up, I told them you weren't active anymore."

Mom snarled, "What do you mean, *'when his name came up'*? It didn't float down from the sky. *You* brought it up."

Mr. Taylor shook his head and held out his hands. "You know what I mean, Pete. I told them you were a math teacher, nothing political in that. There was nothing . . . I told them . . . I swear . . . I said you couldn't tell them anything of interest to them. . ." His voice trailed off. "They said they wouldn't bother you. . . . I am so sorry." He stared at his open hands as if they belonged to someone else. "Please believe me, Pete." He looked up at Dad. "We've been friends a long time, haven't we? I . . . I tried to protect you."

Dad stood up and left the room. Grandma went over to the door. "Mr. Taylor," she said, as she held it open.

I don't remember dreaming anything. The nightmare started after I got up. The newspaper was on the table. Front page, sitting there.

Dad was in the kitchen making coffee when I came in. Mom was still in bed. Dad looked up at me and smiled.

"How can you be so . . . so calm?" I said. He reached over to me, but I pulled away. "I mean it. How can you?"

"Jamie, sweetheart, it'll be all right, I promise you."

He couldn't promise anything. I knew that. I'm not dumb. I felt wildly afraid. I'm going to be like Harriet. I stepped back. "I'll buy me and Stevie lunch today," I said without looking at him. "Stevie," I hollered down the hallway, "meet you on the stoop."

I sat on the bottom step. Barry came out and started to say something, but Charlie was right behind him.

"Hey, Jamie, the Legion's thinking 'bout taking back that award."

"Zip it, Charlie. You couldn't write a winning essay even if your father was J. Edgar Hoover himself."

Barry turned away, and Charlie smirked. "Hey, Barry, watch out the red stain don't rub off on you." Charlie cocked his finger like a gun at Barry and walked away.

Barry kicked a bottle cap. He stared at the sidewalk. "My mom says she's gonna invite you all for dinner tonight, but I . . . I got basketball practice. See ya."

I nodded. I watched him walk away and then I remembered basketball practice is on Tuesdays. This is Thursday. When Stevie came down, we walked the whole way in silence and then went up separate staircases.

I picked up the mimeographed assignment sheet from the pile on Mr. Bracton's desk, and he looked up at me.

"There's a Morse in the paper this morning, Jamie. Related to you?" Was he kidding? My ears started ringing. Three kids already in their seats turned to look at me.

"Yes. My dad."

Mr. Bracton turned away quickly and began to do something with his files.

Seems I've learned how not to lie overnight. I sat down at my desk. The rest of the staff dribbled in. Iris came down my aisle. Her desk was a couple behind me. She stopped for a second and smiled, or maybe I imagined it. Nothing seemed steady. Her face melted into Charlie's. Then, like the Cheshire cat, it slowly faded away except for Charlie's grin. I gripped the sides of my desk, but it bent like rubber in my hands. I felt myself slipping down.

When I opened my eyes, the school nurse was peering down at me. "Did you eat breakfast, Jamie?"

"Sure," I said. Then I remembered I'd rushed out with only my books and allowance money. "No." I looked around. "What am I doing here?" I sat up and moved my legs off the couch.

"Sit still," she said, and handed me a cup of orange juice and a cracker. "Eat it. You're staying here until I say you can leave." She promised she'd get Stevie's lunch money to his room.

I moved over to the table and pulled out my books. We're reading *Alice's Adventures in Wonderland*.

"Jamie Morse?" One of the secretaries from the principal's office stood in the doorway. "Mr. MacGregor wants to see you." The nurse nodded and told me to leave my stuff.

Why would the principal want to see me about missing breakfast? I'd only been in Mr. MacGregor's office once before, when I was called down and told I'd won the "I Am an American" essay contest. You're called in for prizes or detention. And fainting?

Mr. MacGregor was going through a pile of papers. When he saw me, he leaned back in his chair and began tapping his fingertips together. I stared at his tiny white hands.

Tap, two, three, four. *Tap*, two, three, four. I was afraid I'd be hypnotized. If I went into a trance, me the nonliar, who knows what I'd say. Not that I could think of any important secrets left to tell. I tore my eyes away from his fingers, and that's when I saw the newspaper on the right side of his desk. It was folded open to *the* article, the Morse family history.

"I understand you were taken to the nurse's office earlier. Is that correct?"

What a dumb question. He'd sent someone there to get me. He pulled his chin down and squinted at me over the top of his glasses. A shaft of sun glinted through the window and bounced off the bald circle in the middle of his head.

"Young lady, did you hear me?"

"Yessir. Sorry, sir. Yessir, I was in the nurse's office, sir."

He cleared his throat. "Well young lady, Mr. Bracton says there are too many people in the room—" His voice got lower and lower. I wish he wouldn't call me "young lady." Something bad always happens when someone says that.

"—a new homeroom."

"I . . . I don't understand, sir."

He moved the paper from the right to the left side of his desk. "What don't you understand?" he said. "I just told you you're going into a new homeroom. Mr. Bracton says you've completed your *NB* assignment. Halloween, wasn't it?" I nodded, but he didn't look up. "Mr. Bracton needs layout space. He needs to free up desks . . ."

I direct the cameraman to focus on his head. The bald circle fills the lens. He lifts his head. Camera moves in for a tight shot. Mouth fills the screen. Lips open and close like an incinerator door. He's saying something, but there's no sound. Only the clicking of teeth.

". . . Mr. Bracton needs a bigger space." Mr. MacGregor peered at me.

What did he mean? Was he taking away my desk? "But, sir, I'm fine. I just didn't have breakfast. That's all. I'm fine, really I am."

"I'm sure you are," he said to the window.

"I'm still on the paper, right?"

He picked up a pencil. "Check in the office tomorrow morning for your new homeroom assignment."

"Please, Mr. MacGregor . . ."

He stood up and went out to the secretaries' desks.

In the nurse's office, my books had been moved to the side of the table, but *Alice* lay open to the page I'd been reading. I stared at it. Am I off *NB*? *Off, off, off?* Words were jumbled on the page. When they settled back into sentences, there it was:

"Now, I give you fair warning," shouted the Queen, stamping on the ground as she spoke; "either you or your head must be off, and that in about half no time! Take your choice!"

This wasn't my choice! I shouted back at the queen. This was my dad's choice. His fault! My eyes started to burn.

I'm out of the homeroom, Mr. MacGregor said, but *NB* staff are always in the homeroom. Like Mom's books, replaced by bric-a-Bracton. *Kicked off*, he just didn't say it.

In the back of the nurse's office some kid was coughing and spitting into a cup. I left. I felt red hot behind my eyes. Anger hot.

"WE HAVEN'T heard from George," Mom said in the morning. Grandma started humming. Mom stared at her. "What, Mama? What are you trying to tell me?"

"I wouldn't hold my breath."

Mom threw up her hands. "You don't think George is going to call? Pete is his brother, for heaven's sake."

I made Stevie and me sandwiches for lunch, and we hurried out.

You never expect the sun to be shining on a miserable day, but the sky was already a sharp blue. Barry didn't meet us on the stoop.

"No Barry," I muttered. "Some friend."

"I bet he's still sick," Stevie said.

I haven't told him about Barry's basketball practice excuse. "Maybe," I said.

"He's okay." Stevie pressed hard on his cowlick.

"Maybe." And I haven't told him or anybody about NB.

"Have you ever seen the Purdy Street gang?" he asked.

"Don't be ridiculous," I said, and poked him hard.

"But they're in the neighborhood, right?"

"I don't even know if there is a Purdy Street, let alone a gang. So forget it." He wasn't satisfied with that answer. Me neither.

Word is out. Kids in the hallway were parting like the Red Sea to let me pass. At lunchtime, I got an order of French fries from the hair nettles and looked for Elaine. I didn't see her. Gail Boseman and her club of girls giggled as I walked by. I knew it was about me. My ears burned, and I almost didn't hear my name.

"Hey, Jamie, over here." Brian Powser motioned to me. Paul Shapiro was sitting with him. The outcasts, and I'm going to sit with them. Not because I'm brave. I'm one of them. Uncle Joe would be embarrassed I'm his niece.

"Hey, guys." I sat down next to Brian. He was picking

the fried part off a French fry. "What's the point?" I asked.

He shrugged. "I like it that way."

"Easier than picking off the French," Paul grinned.

I laughed. Then Brian said softly that if he saw me again at Mrs. Manny's newsstand, he'd say hello.

I nodded and took a deep breath. "I guess we're the three Reds."

"Oh, he's not," Brian said, pointing his elbow at Paul. "He's just a friend."

I stared at Paul. "You mean you're sitting here even though . . ." I didn't know how to finish the sentence.

Paul shrugged. "No big deal," he said.

I looked away. I missed Elaine.

Herbie from my building walked over to our table with a carton of chocolate milk and his lunch in a bag.

"Hi, guys," he nodded at Brian and Paul. I guess he sits with them. I never noticed because I'm usually with Elaine. He sat down in the seat next to me. Three outcasts, and one friend.

"Charlie was calling you and Stevie Commie-pinkos yesterday," he said in an everyday voice.

It is a big deal! I wanted to scream to Paul.

"I told him he was like a parrot—*Squawk! Squawk!*—one line is all he knows." Herbie laughed. "He didn't much like that."

"*Squawk! Squawk!*" Paul imitated.

I started to giggle. And suddenly we were all squawking like crazy. Kids stared at us, but for the first time I didn't care.

The good feeling started to wear off during the afternoon as fewer and fewer people talked to me. It was completely gone by the end of the day. Walking home, I felt like I had concrete slabs in my shoes. Where the heck is Purdy Street, anyway? The closer I got to our building, the heavier each step. By the time I reached the stoop, I felt like I was dragging a body that weighed five million pounds.

Where was Elaine?

I had a bad feeling about going upstairs.

"Sheila, honey, you have to stop crying so I can hear what you're saying." Mom was handing Aunt Sheila a tissue as I came in the door. It sounded like Aunt Sheila was saying, "Green! Green!"

Mom looked relieved when she saw me. "Jamie, sweetheart, would you make us some tea?" she said. "I think we could all use a cup."

When I brought the tea, they were sitting on the couch, and Aunt Sheila was talking in a low voice. She picked apart little pieces of tissue and twisted them into tiny balls that she dropped on the rug.

Mom is usually a nut about that kind of mess, but she sat still, listening. She was holding Aunt Sheila's hand.

"Where do you think he's gone?" Mom asked.

Gone, not green.

Aunt Sheila shook her head. She stood up, walked to the window, and absently pushed at the curtain.

"When Maury called and told us Pete was fired, George went into a tailspin," she said. "I've never seen him like that."

Uncle George? I had thought he would go to Mr. Henry Taylor's apartment, ring the bell, and punch the living daylights out of him.

"He paced back and forth muttering, 'What are we going to do? What's going to happen to us?' over and over."

There was no way I could picture this. Not Uncle George. Not loud, bullying, slinky-eyeballs Uncle George.

"'Your brother needs family right now.' That's what I said to him. But he just sat there. I don't know if he even heard me." Aunt Sheila came back to the couch. "I was so furious, I picked up a book and threw it at him. 'How dare you!' I said. 'Pete is in terrible trouble and all you can think about is you!'" She stopped abruptly, as if shocked at her own outburst.

Mom gave Aunt Sheila a hug. "It's all right," she said. "We all need family now. We'll get through this."

Aunt Sheila started to cry again, and Mom sent me for the tissue box. When I came back, Mom was saying, ". . . and you'll make coleslaw, right? It's good to chop. Carrots and cabbage don't mind being attacked." They both smiled and walked to the front door.

I went into my room. Where was Elaine? I had this crazy desire to race over to her apartment and bang on her door.

Stevie came in. His knee was cut and he had a scrape on his elbow. "You want me to get Mom?" I said. He shook his head. "What happened?"

He shrugged. "They came after me."

"Who?"

"Andy and Stewie and Creepo Charlie, that's who," he said.

He ran into his room, and I followed him. I let him cry for a minute. "Hey, listen," I said. "Now's when you find out who your real friends are." Stevie kept wiping his eyes. "That's what counts. You know what I mean?"

He shook his head.

"Listen, who's Charlie anyway? He's just a bully."

"He's big."

A man's hand is raised high. The camera follows the downward blow as the belt slices the air. Whack! The boy clenches his fists against his eyes. Cut to the school-yard. The boy turns his head like a radar beam. Searching. He marches over to a little kid and pushes him to the ground. Punches him. He smiles. His fists unball.

"Charlie's a jerk," I said. "Forget him." Then I told him about Barry.

Stevie chewed his lower lip. "I'm going to come home by Linwood Street from now on. Nobody'll follow me there," he said.

"Why not?"

"'Cause I wrote a note saying, 'Purdy Street gang near Linwood,' and stuck it in the schoolyard fence during recess. Stewie found it." Stevie smiled. "Good diversion, right?"

"The best," I said.

Suddenly I was furious at Dad. The kid can't walk home without getting chased. Couldn't Dad see what he was doing to us?

Aunt Sheila came back a little after Dad got home. Still no Uncle George. Nobody said much. Stevie and I had our secrets, and from the looks of it, so did everybody else. Dad was pale.

"He's at McGovern's down at the Oval," Aunt Sheila said.

Did she mean the bar and grill next to the Palace?

"Jamie, Stevie, homework." Mom sent us away.

I left my door open, but they were talking too softly for me to hear anything. Stevie came in and lay down on the rug. He brought his arithmetic homework. He wrote and erased about a dozen times. "What do you think they're talking about?"

"Seems Uncle George is hanging out at McGovern's," I said.

"Why?"

"I don't know. Maybe he got in a fight with Mr. Dirty Rat Taylor, and he got beat up and is drowning his sorrows at McGovern's." *"Drowning his sorrows"* was this great line from a movie we once saw about a private eye who had his own detective agency.

Stevie grinned. "Yeah, sure," he laughed. *"Drowning his sorrows."* It was a ridiculous thought, and we both felt better.

"Get your jacket," I said to him. "Private eye time."

I told Mom we were going to the lobby. Kids from the building hang out there all the time.

We walked toward the Oval and the Palace. When we got to McGovern's, I tried to look in the windows, but the glass was frosted like a bathroom. Stevie was behind me when I pushed open the door. The smell of stale beer was overwhelming, and you could barely see for all the smoke. But there he was, Uncle George, sitting at the bar, his head bobbing up and down.

"Drowning," Stevie whispered. We fled back out.

When we got home Aunt Sheila was already gone. Later that night, the phone rang. I listened at Mom and Dad's bedroom door. It was forever before Dad hung up. "Sheila. The bartender called her," Dad said. "She went to McGovern's, but George sent her away."

I went back to bed and pulled the cover over my head.

ONE DAY last year, Gail Boseman invited me to her house. "Hey, Jamie," she said. "Come over after school. Me and the girls are thinking about letting you into the club." I didn't say anything to Elaine about it. I figured I'd tell her after, but I didn't have to. None of those girls ever spoke to me again after that one time. I guess I didn't pass. So what.

So what is this. In homeroom today before the teacher came in, Gail wrote, "Saturday—4:30!" on the board. "Remember to bring your invitation," she said. "You need it for the door prize."

It seemed everybody knew what she was talking about. From the way some kids glanced at me, Gail must have told everybody I wasn't invited.

At lunch, I looked around for Elaine, but couldn't find her. I sat down with Brian and Paul and Herbie. Herbie's in my new homeroom, and even he was invited to Gail's party.

Social studies after lunch. Before class started, Mrs. Ridit called me up and said she liked all my quotes in the Hollywood paper. I'm crossing my fingers she won't call on me. After Gail Boseman's invitation mess in homeroom, I don't need anybody else looking at me. I figure maybe Mrs. Ridit will leave me alone, since we're off Hollywood and reading now about the peoples of the Amazon River basin.

"Jamie Morse." Mrs. Ridit said my name through her nose, like a bull snorting. "Enlighten us on the plight of the peasants in the Amazon River basin."

Maybe it was Gail, maybe it was getting kicked off *NB*, I don't know, but I burst like the Grand Coulee Dam.

"I don't know about Amazon peasants and I don't even know about peasants in the Soviet Union."

She looked startled.

"Peasants and everybody else should be treated fairly, and progressive people care about fairness . . . and my mother organized a collection for a family on the North Side when the landlord put all their furniture on the street"—I couldn't believe I was talking about this—"and my parents signed a petition to get a Negro family into our building . . . my Uncle Maury organized that and I was on the picket line in front of the landlord's office with them. . . and . . . and . . ."

My mind was racing to figure out what to say next, but my mouth didn't wait. It kept on going.

". . . and in Holland you can be a member of any political party, even the Communist Party, and Holland's been around a lot longer than us . . . and it's just plain selfish if you don't think about anybody but yourself. . . ."

I felt like a rocket that had blasted off a planet of lies into a new universe. I felt woozy.

Charlie hooted. Mrs. Ridit stood with her mouth open.

Elaine sat still as a stone. Embarrassed, I bet, because everybody knew she was my friend. Or at least used to be.

When the bell rang, I followed after Elaine, but she was already halfway down the hall.

Paul caught up with me. "That was interesting, Jamie."

I barely heard him. I couldn't believe Elaine left like that.

"Your family sounds nice," he said.

It sank in, what he was saying. I turned to face him. "Nice? You mean weird, don't you?"

He smiled.

I started to laugh. "I think my family's one big mess," I said.

"Hey, you should see my room."

Elaine's wrong. Paul's not so serious. I don't know what made me think of it, but I said, "Did you ever have Mr. Tubell?"

He shook his head.

"You would have liked him. He had a great mustache."

"I heard he dyed it."

"I bet Mr. Tubell's in some place like Minnesota and I bet he roots for the Brooklyn Dodgers."

"Jackie Robinson's a great left fielder," Paul said as he headed for his next class.

I wonder if Elaine will ever talk to me again. I had slipped a note into her locker first thing this morning to tell her this week's Fettleson show was Mom's. I invited her over to listen with us. No reason to keep the house a secret place now. I'll tell her Grandma is much better. The last big lie.

"My dad says I can't be friends with you anymore."

I hadn't even heard her come up next to me.

"So I can't come for the show," Elaine said, as she crumpled up my note.

She walked away.

Can't be friends with me.

When I got home, Mom was sitting real still in the throne chair, and Dad was pacing up and down, with Uncle Maury going in the opposite direction. Grandma sat in the rocking chair, not moving.

"Your mother has been fired," Dad said.

"Me too."

Mom looked up. They all stared, waiting for me to explain. "Yeah, well, I . . . the principal called me in the other day and told me I was out of the *NB* homeroom, and I know it wasn't because I fainted, but because of the article in paper and—"

"What do you mean 'fainted'?" Dad said.

I explained about skipping breakfast and ended up telling them about the Red Sea parting of kids in the hallway when I go from class to class.

Dad stopped pacing and stood quite still in the middle of the living room. "We are going out to dinner," he said. "They are not going to take over our lives."

Aunt Sheila came over, alone, and we all went to Mario's Italian Cuisine.

"Did they fire you right when you came in?" Stevie asked Mom. "Who did it? Did anybody say anything?"

He was shooting out questions like he was pitching pennies.

"What'd you say when they told you? Did you clean out all the newspapers? Was anybody nice?"

Mom sighed. "Just before lunch," she said, "my boss called me into his office."

Like me and the principal.

"He said they'd been getting calls from the main advertiser on the show, who's threatening to pull out if I continue to write scripts."

"But the advertiser makes soap bars," I said. "Why do they care about you?"

"Bastards!"

"Enough, Maury," Mom said. She looked at Stevie and me. "It could be a lot worse. I could have been one of the actors, with everybody knowing my voice. At least I can still write."

"Will you change your name?" Stevie asked.

"If I have to."

"How about Itskowitz?" I said, and we all laughed. "Hey, Dad, maybe you could write too." He looked at me, his eyes soft. In that second, I wished my arms were six feet long so I could wrap them around both him and Mom and give them a big hug. I wanted Mom to work on her Loony file and Dad on his crossword puzzles. Our normal.

18

THIS JOINT'S *quiet like a morgue.* Private eye movie. That's our house, quiet like a morgue. Dad's in the living room when we go to school in the morning, and he's usually there when we get home. He has a pile of books next to his chair and a pad and a couple of pens. If I don't have a lot of homework, I go back downstairs and hang out until it gets dark.

Sometimes I walk up and down different blocks. It's four days since I'm off *NB*, but it feels like forever. I walk a lot. Only thing I've met is a stray kitten, orange-colored, hanging around the schoolyard.

There's an empty bowl wedged partly under the fence, so I guess somebody's been putting out food scraps. Two days ago I saw a couple of high school boys flinging stones at it. I yelled at them and rattled the fence real hard to warn the kitten. The boys laughed and called me crazy. But the kitten got away.

We're not allowed pets in our building, otherwise I'd take it home. The landlord's got to be a creep to have a rule like that. Big deal, you keep your dog on a leash so it won't mess up the sidewalks, and cats don't go outside anyway. A couple of years ago when I wanted a puppy, I asked Mom to complain, but she said you have to pick carefully what you fight about. "Conserve your strength for the big battles," she said. Pets seemed pretty big to me. So I copied the address off the rent envelope and wrote the landlord myself. Never got an answer. I guess he didn't think it was a big battle either.

It wasn't dark yet, and so I kept on walking. I couldn't believe it. There they were again. "Hey, you! Pick on somebody your own size!" Those creepos had a belt tied around the kitten's hind legs and were hanging it from the fence.

"Wanna see my curve?" one of them said as he threw a ball at the kitten. I ran down the block, lowered my head, and rammed into his side. He pushed me away. "Hey, you a nutcase, or something?"

One of the boys grabbed me from behind and shoved me down on the sidewalk. Somebody spit on me, and I heard them all laugh. "Aw, just a dumb girl. Let her go."

I rolled out of their way. They looked like they were going to start throwing that ball again. I got up and ran home.

"Dad! Dad, you've got to stop them! You've got to!" I was panting, and the words weren't coming out in sentences. "The schoolyard! Those boys! The kitten!"

Without a word he got up. No wasted time on questions. No wasted time at the elevator. Down the stairs. Out the door and down the stoop. I ran ahead, screaming, "Stop it! Stop it!" The boys started to laugh again.

"Here she comes, the crazy girl." Then they must have seen Dad, because they turned and ran off.

I untied the belt. The kitten's eyes were wild, but it seemed to know I wanted to help. It whimpered. Under its cries I could also hear purring. I started to cry. Dad put his arms around me.

"Dr. Stone," he said. "He's a veterinarian across the Oval. We'll take this little one there."

One of the kitten's back legs flopped loosely, as if pulled out of its joint. "How can it cry and purr at the same time?" I said.

"Let me see." Dad took the kitten and put his ear

to its head. "It's purring all right." And he smiled.

When we got to Dr. Stone's office, I couldn't believe it. Mrs. Ridit was sitting in the waiting room, with a cat carrier by her side. She had on a big sweater and skirt, nothing like the belted dresses she wears to school. And her hair wasn't neat. Strands hung around her face, as if she'd gone out without looking in the mirror. She seemed irritated when we came in.

"Jamie Morse," she said coldly. Then she saw the cat in Dad's arms. No more the Mrs. Ridit I knew. She moved faster than I've ever seen her. "What happened? Poor little thing." She gently touched its head, and looked at me, waiting for an answer. When I didn't answer, she looked at Dad.

"Some older boys who apparently take pleasure in torturing something defenseless." He said it quietly. Mrs. Ridit nodded, her mouth in a grim line. Mrs. Ridit? Agreeing with Dad? Next thing I knew, she'd gotten a cup of water from Dr. Stone's bathroom. She wet her finger and offered it to the kitten. A sniff, and then a tiny pink tongue started licking.

"I'm going to find out who did this," she said in the old Mrs. Ridit voice.

The door opened, and Dr. Stone motioned to her. "We're only getting a booster shot," she said. "Why don't you take them first?"

"He's going to be okay," I told her when we came out.

"Maybe a limp, but Dr. Stone says even that may go away."

"Do you know the boys who did this?"

I shook my head. She looked sternly at me. "This is not about movie star pictures," she said.

"I don't." I looked up at Dad. "Really, I don't."

"I believe, Mrs. Ridit, that if Jamie knew and didn't want to tell you, she wouldn't, but she wouldn't say she didn't know." He paused. "She's not a liar, Mrs. Ridit."

Mrs. Ridit looked at me. "This is Charlotte," she said, pointing to her cat carrier. And then she walked into Dr. Stone's examining room.

"What's going to happen to the kitten?" I asked Dad. "Maybe if we bring him home in a closed box and don't ever let him go near the window, the landlord won't know we have him."

Dad listened to me babble on. Finally he said, "But it wouldn't be any fun for a cat, would it? Can't look out at the world, and it would have to be careful not to purr too loudly." That made me smile. "I'm sure Dr. Stone will find a home for him," Dad said. "He's never had any trouble placing orphans like this little one."

"Dumb cat got caught," Charlie said. He looked at us from the front of the room. We were all waiting for the second bell and Mrs. Ridit. "Moral of the story.

Don't hang out where you're not wanted." He laughed. Charlie slid into his seat just as Mrs. Ridit came in the room. On the blackboard he'd drawn a picture of a cat's head looking through a fence. Its whiskers were turned down.

"Who did that drawing?" Mrs. Ridit asked. Charlie grinned. Mrs. Ridit has always liked Charlie's drawings. She left his rocket ship with an American flag on the side board for two days.

"Up here this minute," she said. Charlie looked puzzled. "What do you know about the cat and the fence?"

Mrs. Ridit likes Charlie, everybody knows that. But I know how much she loves cats. Charlie looked uncomfortable.

"Not much," he said. "Just what I heard."

"And what was that?"

Charlie shrugged. "Some cat leaving a mess where it shouldn't. Teaching it a lesson." He paused. "I guess."

I've never seen Mrs. Ridit so angry. Not even when she was upset about the U.N. Suddenly Charlie looked scared. "Don't really know anything," he mumbled.

Mrs. Ridit glanced at me and then back at Charlie. "Detention for the rest of the week. And report to the principal's office at the end of this class."

"But I didn't—"

"Wait for me in the office."

Wowee, Charlie getting detention. Let him stew, the bully.

The rest of the class period I kept thinking about Charlie. I can spot him a block away, and I know he wasn't there. But why should I help him? Think about things that make you smile and you'll have sweet dreams, that's what Grandma always says. Well, Charlie getting detention is going to give me very sweet dreams.

"Can we check on Moxie?" I asked Dad. That's what I'd named the tough little cat. It was three and a half days since we'd found him. Every day I'd come home, and every day Dad would be sitting in the living room. Staring or reading. "Moxie, the kitten, can we check on him?"

Dad looked up. "Gives you a good feeling, that name, doesn't it?" he said, folding up his paper.

We crossed the Oval. I skipped every other step to keep up with him. "We'll just make it," Dad said. I ran ahead.

Mrs. Bennet, the assistant, was behind the front desk when we came in. "Doing just fine," she told us.

"I named him Moxie," I said.

She smiled. "Go on in. Our last patient left, and Doc is straightening up."

"This little guy is dragging that cast around," Dr. Stone said. "We can't keep him still now that he's got free run of the place. He's your basic explorer."

I squatted down, and Moxie charged over to me. Well, hobbled. He started purring before he even reached me. "Moxie's his name," I said, as I rubbed behind his ears.

"Well, Moxie's going to be the office cat," Dr. Stone said. "I've decided we need a rascal around here." Before I could say anything, he added, "And you've got visiting rights anytime."

When we walked out, Mrs. Bennet was on the phone. "Bring Charlotte right in. No problem. We always leave emergency time at the end of the day. It's absolutely not a problem."

Dad and I walked home in silence until we crossed the Oval into our quadrant.

"Did Mrs. Ridit ever find out who did it?"

I didn't say anything.

"She seemed determined."

I stared at my feet. Skip. Step. Skip. "She thinks Charlie did it," I said at last.

"But you told her he wasn't one of them."

Two skips. I moved a little ahead.

"Jamie?"

"Well, I don't know for sure he wasn't. I didn't get a good look at all of them. I mean, it could have been Charlie."

"But was it? That's really the only question, isn't it?"

I kicked a bottle cap three full sidewalk squares. Neither of us said anything until we reached our stoop. Charlie was hanging out. Dad went upstairs, but Charlie stood in front of me when I tried to pass.

"I saw Mrs. Ridit looking at you. You tell her I did something to that dumb cat?"

I wanted to punch him. "Far as I'm concerned you can get detention for life."

"But I didn't do it. Besides, the dumb cat got what it deserved."

"You're the one got what you deserve."

"I didn't touch it. It's not fair."

I stared at him. "Charlie Nathan worried about fairness?"

"I didn't do anything," he said stubbornly. Then his shoulders sagged. "I didn't do anything."

"Look, you jerk. One thing I'm not is a rat." And I pushed past him.

MOXIE WAS great, but I still had school every day. I ate alone today and went out to the yard before the period ended. I stared through the fence at a lady pushing a baby carriage. A man with a briefcase walked by. Today there'd be an *NB* meeting after school. They were always on Tuesdays. Minus me.

I turned around and headed back inside, writing a letter in my head.

To the NB *Editors: Here's breaking news for* News Breaks. NB *Staffer Disappears from Homeroom. Are you going to send out a reporter to cover this story?*

Sounds too much like a kidnapping.

Rewrite: *Why was a staffer who shall remain name-less ordered out of the* NB *homeroom? She never hurt anyone.*

Sounds whiny.

Rewrite: *Why was Jamie Morse "let go" from the* NB *homeroom?*

Add: *Whatever happened to the idea of a free press? Jamie Morse, that's me, was removed from the* NB *homeroom, without any cause and without any hearing to appeal this decision. Is this fair?*

You bet it's not. I ripped out a piece of paper from my notebook and wrote the letter out just like that, "To the editors: Iris Fleming and Nate Winters." And I signed my name. Big. "Jamie Morse." I folded it up and went inside. I slipped the letter through the slots into Iris's locker.

The bell rang, and I headed for art class. I've been working on a cut-out collage, an abstract tree of col-ored papers. "Looks like you're sharpening the points on those leaves," Mr. Pratt said. "Is that the look you want? Prickly?"

"Yup. I'm a prickly tree." He laughed. I didn't.

"I got your note," Iris said the next day. She was alone at a table in the cafeteria. "Wanna sit down?"

I looked around.

"I've got a meeting in about ten minutes," she said. I sat.

"We're going to publish it."

I looked up from my tray. "You're kidding. I mean, that's great."

"Yeah. I argued with Nate, but in the end he agreed you should at least get some kind of hearing."

I unwrapped my sandwich. Suddenly I thought about my first day in the *NB* homeroom. "Remember Mr. Tubell?" I said.

"I miss him."

"Me too."

We both munched on our sandwiches, and then Iris got up to leave. "Hey, Jamie, good luck. I hope you get that hearing."

Two days later *NB* came out. The papers were stacked on a chair in the back of homeroom. I grabbed a copy and turned to the Letters to the Editor page. My letter wasn't there. I felt hot. What a jerk I was to have believed Iris. I tossed the paper on my desk and bent down to put my books on the floor. When I straightened up, I saw the front-page headline: STUDENT DEMANDS HEARING, with an article stating that I was "summarily removed" from the *NB* homeroom with no explanation. Front page! And they included my letter in the article. I turned to the editorials. Three, and the banner over the top one read: STUDENT DESERVES HEARING.

I don't remember much about the rest of that morning, except social studies. At the end of class, Mrs. Ridit handed me an official envelope. Inside was a note: "Report to Mr. MacGregor's office after fourth period."

"I'm on the review board," Mrs. Ridit said.

I stared at her. "I'm really getting a hearing?"

She ignored me. "I expect you to be organized in your presentation. An outburst like the one that happened with the Amazon peasants will not help you." I nodded. Mrs. Ridit may like cats, but this is school.

I left class in a daze and wondered who'd be at the hearing besides Mrs. Ridit and Mr. MacGregor. I missed Elaine, someone I could talk to.

Mr. MacGregor sat at the front end of the long table in his office. Mr. Pratt smiled at me from the window side. I hadn't expected a friendly face. Mrs. Ridit and Mr. Bracton. Of course Mr. Bracton. Dumb of me not to have figured that. He fired me.

I sat at the far end of the table, a mile away from Mr. MacGregor. "Well, young lady," he said shuffling his papers. "It seems you have some questions?"

My brain was blank, but my mouth started to work. "Why did Mr. Bracton fire me?" This was so weird, not knowing what you were going to say.

"Speak up, young lady," Mr. MacGregor said. "We can't hear you."

"Why did Mr. Bracton fire me?"

Mr. Bracton coughed like he was choking, and I knew absolutely my firing had nothing to do with anything I'd written.

"I've always finished my assignments. And I haven't complained about the deadlines."

"In fact you're not much of a talker are you?" Mr. Pratt said. He turned to the others. "Hardly says anything in art class."

They all stared at me, except Mr. Bracton.

"Did she do anything that violated the paper's rules?" Mrs. Ridit asked. She looked at Mr. Bracton. He looked at the window.

Mr. MacGregor twisted a pencil. He tapped it on the table. "We've a space problem," he said. "Isn't that right, Herbert?"

Everybody looked at Mr. Bracton, who cleared his throat and stared at the papers in front of him. "Without a larger homeroom, we can't easily do the layouts. We need an extra desk."

"But why Jamie?" Mr. Pratt said. "That's the question, isn't it?"

"If there's tension in that homeroom, it affects the smooth running of the operation," Mr. MacGregor said. He sounded irritated. "Isn't that what you told me, Herbert?"

We all turned to Mr. Bracton.

"The staff feels they can't count on Jamie," Mr. Bracton said. "She's not really been part of the group." His voice got stronger. "She doesn't fit in."

"What's to fit in?" Mr. Pratt asked. "If she does her assignments—"

"But it is important to fit in," Mr. Bracton said. "That keeps everything running smoothly. Avoids conflict."

Mr. MacGregor sighed. "The paper is a flagship for the school," he said. "What are we telling the parents of other students if we allow someone to introduce tension on the staff?"

"Someone to introduce tension?" Mr. Pratt repeated. "This is Jamie Morse, and so far I haven't heard anyone say anything about her writing or how she causes tension." He paused and leaned back. "If you're worried about parents, you're saying this is really about the news articles on her father. Isn't that right?"

Mrs. Ridit's eyes narrowed.

"But *he's* not on *NB*," I said.

They stared at me and began to talk all at once, as if something had been dropped on the table that they had to cover up real fast.

Mrs. Ridit's mouth was tight. She turned to me and stared as if she was juggling something inside her head. "What exactly have you written for the paper?" she said finally.

"I wrote the piece about the Halloween assembly, and—"

"Halloween?" she said, her right eyebrow shot up. "What else?"

"I'd started to work on something . . . I mean, it was going to be this long thing ab—"

"Get to the point, Jamie. What else?"

Mr. Bracton looked like he had a stomachache, and Mr. MacGregor played with his pencil.

"I was starting to do research for a piece about the first Thanksgiving."

"The first Thanksgiving!" Mr. Pratt exploded. "Where, for heaven's sake, is the tension there?"

Mr. Bracton paled.

"Wait outside," Mr. MacGregor said to me. He turned to the others. "This is getting us nowhere. Does anyone have anything new to say?"

"The editors never said my reporting was bad."

"Please, Jamie. Outside."

I closed the door behind me. Maybe I was mixed up about lots of stuff, but this whole thing was unfair. I sat on the bench across from the office counter. I could hear voices raised inside, but I couldn't make out what they were saying. Then everything went quiet.

I'd said it was wrong not to give me a hearing, and they gave me one. It was the weirdest thing, as if I'd come through a pitch-black hallway into light.

The buzzer rang on the office secretary's desk. "Yes, sir. I'll tell her." She put down the phone. "Go to your next class, Jamie."

"But what about—?"

She shook her head. "I'm sure Mr. MacGregor will talk to you at the appropriate time."

When I got to art class, everybody was waiting for Mr. Pratt. I went to the flat files, took out my tree, and laid it out on my desk. I stared at it. I couldn't remember what I had been doing or why.

"Are you finished with it?" A voice breaking through the fog. Arthur, the kid I share an art table with. His stuff is terrific.

"Yeah. Well, maybe a little extra darkness on this side." I pointed to a branch that twisted upward. "Just to make it stand out a little more."

Arthur cocked his head. "If you darken below the branch, you'll make the eye move up to see the twist. You don't need to darken the branch itself."

I followed his finger. "I see what you mean. Like throwing a spotlight from an angle."

"That's right." He smiled. "You're good with

words." Arthur went back to his side of the table.

Everybody had their projects out. That's how Mr. Pratt works. He'd said the first day that he assumed people were in this class because they wanted to be, and so he didn't see any need to say the obvious, like, "Take out your work."

I love this room. Lots of light through the tall windows, and Mr. Pratt keeps the shades up. We work at long tables with two students at each. You have lots of room to spread out.

When Mr. Pratt came in, the talking stopped, and we started working. He made the rounds, spending a few minutes with each of us. About ten minutes before the end of class, he reached our table. When he finished talking to Arthur, he came over to my end. "Nice how you've pulled our attention here." He pointed to the twisted branch. Before I had a chance to say anything, he said, "See me after class." He walked to the front of the room. "Flat files, everybody."

We lined up to put away our pieces, and I went back to my table. I couldn't focus on anything. There was no clue in "See me after class." Suddenly I felt like laughing hysterically, and nothing was the least bit funny. Dad fired. Mom fired. Me fired. Me . . . ?

The bell rang, and when everyone had left, I made my way slowly up to Mr. Pratt's desk. He was writing in his notebook. He looked up. "We've solved the problem. *NB* needs layout space, and we've got it." He gestured around the room at the long wide tables. He turned to me and smiled. "You're back in the homeroom."

"But it wasn't really about space, was it? It was my father."

Mr. Pratt closed his notebook. "You're back, Jamie," he said softly. "Isn't that enough?"

I walked to my locker. Elaine stood there, looking around nervously. When she saw me coming, she motioned me to hurry up. "The yard," she whispered. We pushed past kids in the hall and went down the side doorsteps that led to the corner yard. Nobody usually hangs out there. It's a narrow strip of cement framed by the building and the school fence. Elaine headed to the farthest corner. "You're not going to believe this." She lowered her voice even though no one was around. "I had to take an envelope to the faculty lounge just before last period."

I stared at her.

She licked her lips. "I was looking for Mr. Martin, but you couldn't miss Mr. Pratt. He was laughing up a storm." She leaned closer to me. "He was telling Mrs. Jenkins about Mrs. Ridit."

"For gosh sake, Elaine, what are you talking about?"

She grinned. "These were his exact words, and I

quote: 'You should have seen Thelma Ridit! Like a bull, she snorted, lowered her head, and charged.'" Elaine looked at me as if she herself couldn't believe what she was saying.

"He said she went after Mr. MacGregor and Mr. Bracton, and if she could've leapt over the table, she would've. Something about you and subversives and Halloween and Thanksgiving."

I could hardly believe it.

"And, according to Mr. Pratt, Mrs. Ridit said—" Elaine's eyes got big—"'You don't punish the child for the sins of the father.'"

"Mrs. Ridit said that?"

Elaine nodded.

We stood for a moment, neither of us saying a word. Then I think we both remembered we weren't supposed to be talking anymore.

"I . . . I just thought you'd want to know," she said.

"Yeah, thanks."

She turned toward the main yard, stopped, and looked back at me. "I'm sorry, Jamie," she said, almost whispering. "See you."

See you? I felt the tiniest bit like smiling.

When school let out, I ran the eight blocks home. *I'm back! I'm back on* NB! And maybe Elaine's my friend again.

"What are you so happy about?" Charlie stood in front of the stoop like he owned it.

"Wouldn't you like to know." I sailed past him. I wasn't even mad at him. He looked short, and I was back.

Dad was in his chair in the living room, writing on a pad. "I'm back on *NB*," I said. He looked up. "I wrote a letter about a hearing, and they gave me one. I won!"

"Well done, Jamie. Congratulations." He smiled, but his eyes looked sad.

I felt a stab. "You never got a hearing."

"Ah," he said. "I don't think they want to hear me say one more word. Ever."

There were columns of numbers on his pad, and in a flash I understood. Money. I hugged him. I think we were both a little surprised. It's not something I do with Dad.

"I'm proud of you," he said.

And suddenly I remembered the last time he had said those same words.

"Dad, do you remember the Stillwells?" He looked puzzled. "The family with the furniture on the street, and we helped put everything back."

"Sure."

It must have been four years ago. The Stillwells had been evicted from their apartment because they hadn't paid the rent. Dad and Mom took me to the rally. No big speeches like Uncle George likes to make. Mrs. Marder, she was the only one who talked. "You don't throw people out of their home because they're a little late with the rent." I can still hear her voice. "You work something out," she said. "That's the decent thing to do. Think about it," she'd said. "Could be you someday, and wouldn't you want somebody to care?"

We handed out sheets to people who walked by. Some brushed past muttering, "Leave me alone." One man hurried by me and said, "Go back to Russia," which totally confused me. I said, "I've never been there," but the man was already gone.

Dad had said, "Never respond to anger with anger." I knew he was telling me something important even though I didn't understand it then.

Some people stopped and talked. One of them said, "What a smart little girl. You must be proud of her." And Dad had said, "I *am* proud of her!"

"I remember." Dad smiled at me.

I felt a rush of warmth and a sadness. "We don't do that anymore. It's because of Senator McCarthy, isn't it?"

"Many things, Jamie. People are afraid."

Me too. But then as I felt around inside me, I realized I wasn't so afraid anymore. No more big secrets.

Now just regular ones like everybody else. I laughed. Dad looked at me. And I laughed again. "Something good came out of getting thrown off *NB*." I paused, and all of a sudden I felt terrible. "I'm back, but you're not. I'm sorry, Dad."

"It's okay. I know what you mean," he said. "Everything's above-board now. A kind of freedom."

MOM GETS up early these days. She leaves the house and doesn't come back till after we're home from school. She doesn't say where she's been, and we still haven't heard anything from Uncle George. When I asked Dad about him, he shook his head and said only, "He's having a hard time."

"Put it on the account," Mom said this morning, when she gave me the grocery list. But when I did that last week, the man at Slonim's took out his handkerchief and gave a huge blow.

"All right, dolly," he said to me. "But you tell your mama by the end of the month, no more account." I didn't tell Mom that. It feels too scary to say anything about money. But I'm going to take the Fig Newtons off the shopping list. Nobody eats them except me and Stevie. And no French fries at school today.

The *NB* homeroom was noisy when I came in, but it's a different kind of noise from other classrooms. Kids were talking about work, *NB* work. A few said hi to me. Timmy turned his back. Kind of corny.

Mr. Bracton was at his desk. I handed him the office slip reassigning me to the homeroom. He didn't look up. "Your old seat," was all he said.

As I walked down the aisle, Iris smiled. "Welcome back. You're just in time for new assignments."

The bell rang, and Nate and Iris went to the front. Iris had a file folder, and Nate started writing on the blackboard.

"Okay, drama club rehearsals?" Iris said. Susan raised her hand. Nate wrote her name down.

"Farewell assembly for Mrs. Denton?" Mrs. Denton made up the cafeteria menus and supervised the nettles. Nobody volunteered. "Selma? How about it?" Nate said. Selma groaned, but nodded.

"Current events roundup?"

"I'll do it."

"Jamie," Nate wrote on the board.

After the assignments were given out, we had an *NB* class period. I felt nervous about the roundup, but ready. I think.

"You sure you want to do this?" Iris said. She motioned me to one of the tables in the back of the room. "I mean, what with everything that's happened—"

"Yeah. I do. Ever since I got the hearing, I feel like I have to find out more about Senator McCarthy."

"Hey, it's okay with me if you want to make that most of the story, but the roundup isn't only about Senator McCarthy."

I showed her a notebook I'd started. "I'm keeping all my notes in here."

"Like any good reporter."

I smiled. Iris was okay. "You know Mrs. Finley at the public library?"

"Sure."

"When I told her I couldn't find anything about Senator McCarthy in all these articles on the House Un-American Activities Committee, she almost bit my head off. 'He is a *senator*, young lady. Why would he be on a committee of the *House of Representatives*?' I felt like such a jerk!"

Iris giggled. "She's tough. But she is terrific when you really need help."

"I guess."

Just then Timmy came over. "Hey, Jamie, doing the roundup so you can defend your father?"

"Shut up, Timmy," Iris said. "You don't know what you're talking about."

But Timmy didn't want to listen. "Russia's got the bomb," he said, "and Communist spies in our government showed them how to make it. That's what my father says."

"Yeah, well, my mother says 'nigger' is a bad word, and that's why we say, 'Catch a *tiger* by the toe.' Now what's that got to do with Russia or bombs or spies?"

Timmy shrugged disgustedly and walked off.

"By the way, I read your Hollywood report," Iris said.

"No kidding?"

"You know how Mrs. Ridit leaves all the reports on the back reading table, well, yours was there. Interesting. The same kind of thing is happening with my dad's union."

I must have looked confused, because she said, "All that stuff about Hollywood producers saying some people are Communists when they don't really know if it's true. That's what my father says about his union."

"But I remember you said in Mr. Tubell's class that your father wasn't in a Communist union."

"He's not, but he says the factory owners want everybody to think all union members are Reds.

That's how they're trying to break the unions."

"You mean, they say people going on strike are trying to overthrow the government?"

"I guess," Iris said. She frowned. "It makes me mad. My father's as much an American as anybody."

"Mine too."

She stared at me for a minute and then nodded. "Gotta go to class," she said. "See you later."

After school I headed for the public library. Mom's list can wait.

The camera opens wide on the schoolyard. A battlefield. The war was started by Mr. Henry Taylor. And Dad's principal. And Mom's boss. And Mr. Bracton. And factory bosses. And Senator Joseph McCarthy and all his pals. This is an MMM production. It takes smarts and luck and guts to dodge the buried grenades, and I have all three. I leap over spots, dodge to the right, twist to the left, charge the center, through the gate. Safe!

I walked over to the reference section.

"Hello, Jamie."

"Hey, Harriet. What are you doing here?"

"It's still my branch." She put her books down at my table.

I hadn't seen Harriet Purdue since I bumped into her at the candy store. And we hadn't talked then. "How's your new school?"

She shrugged. "When they found out why I switched schools, some of the kids were"—she paused—"nasty." She moved around in the chair. "But it's okay," she added quickly. "How about you?"

"Okay. Well, not really." And before I knew it, I was telling her how they kicked me out of the *NB* homeroom, and about Charlie and Gail Boseman and the Red Sea, and how Elaine stopped talking to me. She knew everybody, and listened without interrupting even once.

"And you should have seen it when I erupted in Mrs. Ridit's class," I said. "I told about a million political things my parents had done. Mrs. Ridit changed the subject so fast, you'd think I was Typhoid Mary breathing on everybody." Harriet grinned.

Then I told her about Moxie and Mrs. Ridit and how Mrs. Ridit was part of my getting back on *NB*. I must have been talking loud, because Mrs. Bouncing Glasses Finley came over.

"This is a library." She peered at me. "A quiet place." Then in a change of voice: "Harriet, I'm glad you came in today. Before you leave, come to the desk. I've a book for you." And she walked away.

"Holy mackerel, she actually talks nice to you."

"The first time I came in after we moved," Harriet said, "she told me she was sorry I had to start new classes in the middle of the term. And then she helped me find all the books I needed."

"She's such a grouch-puss with me," I said.

"What are you doing?" Harriet pointed to the pile of books on the table.

"The current events roundup for *NB*."

She made a face. "You'd think they'd give that to someone else. You know . . ."

"I asked for it."

"I hate it."

It was weird hearing Harriet say exactly what I've always said. But something had changed for me.

"I mean, look at this," I said, pointing to a picture in *Time* magazine.

Harriet sat down next to me and we both stared at Senator McCarthy's picture. Here I was, face-to-face with this man who haunted our dinner table.

"He looks like he needs a shave," Harriet said.

She opened her books, and I started to read back issues of *Time* and *Newsweek*.

On February 9, 1950, Senator McCarthy gave his first big speech saying that traitors in the State Department were out to destroy America. In the picture, he was holding up a file. My neck prickled, and I felt as if I was seeing something before it happened.

I kept taking notes. Actress Jean Muir fired from the *The Aldrich Family* show on TV. A suspected Red. Eight junior high and high school teachers on trial in Brooklyn. A college professor, accused of membership in the Communist Party, shot himself. I looked over at Harriet. I wonder if she'd read about that professor.

She was packing up her books and reaching for her coat. "See you, Jamie."

I turned the pages and found myself staring at a photograph that Senator McCarthy had given to the press. In the picture, Senator Tydings, a Democrat, was sitting close to Earl Browder, who the caption said was the former head of the Communist Party in America.

"That was shameful," Mrs. Finley said, as she peered over my shoulder. She tapped her pencil eraser on the magazine picture. "This was supposed to make people think Senator Tydings was sympathetic to Communists."

"They look like they're friends, whispering to each other," I said.

"That's precisely what Senator McCarthy wanted people to believe."

"But you can't just make up a picture."

She pulled off her glasses. "Do you know what 'composite' means?"

"Different pieces?"

She nodded. "These are two separate pictures, cut and pasted together so skillfully, the two men look just as you described them—like friendly associates."

It took me a minute to figure it out. "You mean Senator McCarthy lied to make people think Senator Tydings was a Communist?"

She nodded.

"Wow!"

"Much worse than 'Wow,' my dear."

Me and Senator McCarthy, liars! Only he's saying someone is a Communist who isn't, and I was pretending the opposite. At least I used to. I had to bite my cheek to keep from laughing crazily.

Mrs. Finley sniffed. I looked up at her. "Harriet told me you are in the same situation as she is."

"I guess," I said, looking back down at the magazine. It seems like the whole world knows about the Morse family.

"We give the lie to our own democracy," she said, "if we sacrifice our freedoms to a witch hunt." She paused. "Do you understand?"

I shook my head.

"I have no right to know your father's politics, unless he chooses to tell me." Mrs. Finley's glasses bounced on the chain around her neck. "If everyone in this country doesn't have the right to say what he thinks, we are facing a much greater danger than Senator McCarthy is talking about."

She put her glasses on, and walked back to the front desk.

If I'd thought about it, I'd never have done what I did. I followed Mrs. Finley.

"That's what my dad says."

She nodded. "What is going on in America today is shameful." She peered at me. "It's hard to understand how we could have let this happen." And she turned back to her card file.

It's ridiculous, but I felt better.

UNCLE GEORGE is drunk all the time now. Aunt Sheila told Mom he always liked a drink with dinner, but this is different. He goes to McGovern's as soon as it opens at eleven in the morning and doesn't come home for hours. Aunt Sheila doesn't know what to do about it.

Mom had made a huge vat of spaghetti sauce, and when I got home, she sent me over to Aunt Sheila's with two jars. Right after I got there, Uncle George came in. He took off his jacket and dropped it by the door. Boy, did he smell. I don't think he even saw me.

Actually, I don't think he could see much of anything. He banged into the dining-room table, and veered down the hall into the bathroom. When he came out, he shuffled over to the couch.

As he turned to sit down, he unbuckled his pants. They slipped down to his ankles. He tried to sit but missed the couch by nearly a foot. He sat on the floor and pulled off his shirt. He looked exhausted from the effort, and within seconds he curled up and began snoring.

Aunt Sheila stared at him. "Uh huh," she murmured. "Most days he doesn't make it to the bedroom," she said, talking to me like I was Mom. "He comes in, it's a tornado. Look at this." Her arm swept around the room. She grabbed my hand and pulled me to the bathroom. The towels were balled up on the floor and toothpaste was smeared all over the sink. Uncle George must have tried to squeeze it on his toothbrush and missed.

"I'm lucky today," Aunt Sheila said bitterly. "He didn't throw up in the bathtub."

Uncle George, the man with all the answers, the man who thinks he's smarter than everybody else. I can't figure it out. Maybe the louder you yell, the bigger the mess you can be inside.

Aunt Sheila came home with me to eat dinner. You can usually count on Uncle Maury to say something, but tonight he sat quiet like the rest of us.

Mom broke the silence. "I'm in *Red Channels*, Pete." Dad looked up. "I'm on their list." She held up some papers.

"Is that good?" Stevie asked.

"If your name's in a paper, it can't be good, jerko."

"Shut up, Jamie. You think you know everything."

"All I know is, nothing 'Red' is good."

"What I'm saying, Pete," Mom said, "is that all this isn't happening just because of you."

I stared at her. "You mean—"

"I mean they didn't fire me because of Daddy. I'm my own sinner." She had a weird smile.

"Don't make light of this, Rachel," Dad said. He got up and began to pace back and forth.

"What's *Red Channels*?" Stevie asked.

"It's a list published by a couple of former F.B.I. men," she explained. "They named one hundred fifty-one people in radio and television and movies who they say are Communists or fellow travelers. Many station owners will fire you if your name is on it."

"Like the Hollywood blacklist," I said.

"But what did you do to get on the list?" Stevie asked.

Mom patted his cowlick. "I gave money to a group that fights Jim Crow in baseball. They listed my contribution to that group. I guess if you're against discrimination in the ballpark, these people consider you subversive." She was angry now. You see, in our house, we love Jackie Robinson. We'd root for the Brooklyn Dodgers even if we lived in Minnesota.

"But," Mom went on, "the news is not all bad."

Her eyes swept over us. "You are looking at a new children's book author, thank you very much!"

We stared at her.

"I've been working on a project, and today I had lunch with a book editor. Her company has offered me a contract for a story about the exodusters. I . . . am . . . employed," she said, emphasizing each word. "Rachel *Itskowitz*, author."

"Itskowitz!" Stevie said.

"X-O-what?" I said.

"Exodusters. Former slaves who left the South after the Civil War and went west. Their ex-o-dus to freedom."

"West like the cowboys?" Stevie asked.

"Cowboys and pioneers," Mom said. "There were more than twenty thousand Negro pioneers, and many of them lived in little houses on the prairie." Mom turned to me and smiled.

As a little kid I used to pretend I was traveling west in a covered wagon. I'd put a sheet over the card table and flick a whip over oxen. "I can't wait to read it."

"Me too!" Stevie said.

"Me too!" Mom smiled again.

Uncle Maury spoke for the first time. "Watch out," he said. "There's bound to be somebody who'll consider it a danger to our nation's youth to learn that Negroes were a part of the great American movement west." Uncle Maury laughed, "Yes, indeed!"

And so for the first time in many weeks, we laughed in our house. Me included.

22

A FEW days later on the way to school, Stevie and I passed a newsstand with papers piled high. One of the headlines was huge:

McCARTHY ROUTS REDS
SCHOOL HEARINGS SOON

School hearings? My hands felt sweaty, and I had to make myself breathe. I told Stevie to go ahead without me.

I read the story. Senator McCarthy was going to

make "Commie teachers" testify before his committee. A subpoena, the paper called it. A piece of paper saying you have to appear before the committee and talk. You have to tell them what you know. You have to be a "friendly," or go to jail.

I stared at the paper. Someone banged my leg with a shopping bag. I looked up. The Crazy Lady. The belt of her house dress was untied, and she had on a thin sweater, backward. She tapped the fingers of her left hand in the air. Her right arm hung down, the shopping bag dangling from her hand. It was too late to cross the street. She was next to me.

I watched as she fingered the air. She walked on and turned a corner, but I knew she was still there.

Close-up of a hand, moving, stirring. Camera pulls back an inch a second. The Crazy Lady. She is the daughter of my unknown grandfather. When he left his sons, he took her with him. Then she left him, and now she has amnesia. One morning as she glides along the sidewalk, her fingers trace the letters of her name in the air. Shazam! *She remembers everything.*

In real life, Dad doesn't have a sister. But this is my movie. She's my long-lost aunt.

I'd stayed late after school for an *NB* meeting. When I got home, everybody was in the living room.

Dad sat on the throne. He was holding a piece of paper. Aunt Sheila and Uncle Maury were there. And Libby Tollman, Barry's mother, was making coffee. Stevie sat staring at his feet and wouldn't look at me no matter how many times I poked him.

In the kitchen Mom told me that Aunt Sheila had called, distraught about Uncle George. Dad had gone to McGovern's to look for him. Stevie was home alone and was so absorbed in building a diorama for his geography class, he forgot Mom's rule. When the bell rang, he opened the door without thinking. An investigator from the McCarthy committee showed his identification and asked for Dad. When Stevie tried to close the door, the man blocked it and came in.

"He waited," Mom said. "And when Dad returned, the investigator handed him a subpoena for the committee hearings next week."

"A subpoena? Boy, Stevie really did it!" I said.

Mom stared at me. "Come." We walked to the living room, and she took Stevie's hand and brought us both into her room. We sat on the end of the bed. I looked at Mom. Stevie looked at the floor.

Mom closed her eyes and pushed hair away from her forehead, as if clearing a path. "You two," she said so softly I had to lean forward to hear her. "I am so sorry for the secrets." She pulled us to her. "Never again. No matter what."

"But I did it." Stevie's voice cracked.

"Absolutely not!" Mom said. "Absolutely not. If not today, later. They would have delivered that subpoena, Stevie, somehow." She took his chin in her hand. "You did not cause anything."

"McCarthy did."

Mom looked at me. "That's right. Senator McCarthy, and all the people who are afraid to stand up to him."

"Like you said about President Eisenhower?" Stevie asked, finally looking up.

"Even the president," Mom said. She hugged us both. Squooshed in together, it felt good. When she stood up, she said in a tired but clear voice, "No more secrets."

". . . Joe McCarthy," Uncle Maury was saying, when we came back into the living room. He always growls when he says the name.

Dad cleared his throat and looked over at Mom. He didn't look gray or tired. It was as if the subpoena had filled him with a new energy.

Catch a tiger by the toe.

"Senator McCarthy and his committee want something I won't give them." His voice was firm and he smiled at Mom.

Aunt Sheila was crying. My family sat around the

room, like covered wagons drawn together at night in a circle.

During supper the doorbell rang, and Dad turned to Stevie. "Answer it," he said. "Nothing bad is going to happen."

Uncle George stood in the doorway. He was pale, and looked exhausted. He walked over to the table and stood in front of Dad. "I'm with you, Pete," he said. His eyes held some sort of apology. Aunt Sheila moved her chair over, and Uncle George joined us.

I WOKE suddenly and looked at the clock. Four A.M. I groaned, and pulled the cover over my head. Uncle George's words kept going round and round in my head, like a record player with the needle stuck. "I'm with you, Pete. I'm with you, Pete."

But it wasn't enough that Uncle George had come back. Senator McCarthy lurked like a rattlesnake in the tall grass, and Dad had to go out to meet him. I rolled over onto my stomach with the pillow over my head. Then I tossed back around, and the blanket slipped to the floor. I knocked the pillow off the bed when I reached for the blanket.

I decided to go for a glass of water.

Even when I was little, I never believed that monsters hid under the bed waiting to catch bad little boys and girls. Sure, I told Stevie they were there and would chew on his fingers when he fell asleep, but I never believed it. I think I've always known that whatever is scary is right next to you when you're wide-awake.

Dad was in the living room when I padded through. "Can't sleep?" he asked.

I brought two glasses of water from the kitchen, and we sat on the couch. Dad reached over and put his arm around my shoulders. I slid closer to him. Then I remembered something that had bothered me. "Why was Barry's mother here?" I asked.

"She wanted to make sure we understood she's our friend."

"But Barry's not talking to me."

Dad took a sip of water. "I guess he feels he's got to do what the other kids do." Dad gave me a hug. "He'll come around."

"How do you know that?"

"Mrs. Tollman called after she saw the first article and invited us for dinner."

"Barry said something about that. But we never went," I said. "She must have changed her mind."

"We couldn't that night. We will."

I wanted to bang on the kitchen pipe that instant. *"Meet-me-on-the-stoop-you-jerk!"*

"What does the committee want?"

Dad stretched his legs out. "They want from me what they got from Henry Taylor."

I pictured Mr. Taylor sitting on this couch, staring at his hands. "They want you to give them names?"

Dad nodded.

"What happens if you don't?"

"This is where it gets interesting."

This wasn't interesting. It was frightening.

He sat up again. "Anyone should be able to join a group like the one Mom gave money to. 'The right of the people peaceably to assemble.' That's what the First Amendment says."

"The First Amendment?"

Dad reached for me. I pulled away and stared at him, trying to see his face in the dark. "You believed you had a right to a hearing about your school paper. In fact, you demanded it," Dad said.

"That's not the same. That's just school." My mind was racing. "The Hollywood Ten talked about the First Amendment, and they went to prison."

"Just school?" Dad took me by the shoulders. "Don't you see, Jamie? They've given me a hearing, and, like you, I'm not running."

"But I wasn't going to go to prison."

"Jamie, listen to me."

"What if nobody buys Mom's book? What if you're

in prison and we have to move?" My voice cracked.

"We're going to be fine," he said.

"You'll go to prison!" My voice was hoarse. "You will! They'll take you!"

Suddenly I had an idea. "What about Mr. Truett?" I said. "The man you and Mom knew. The man who died. Give them *his* name. It can't hurt him!"

Dad got up and walked over to the window.

"It doesn't matter that Mr. Truett is dead, Jamie. You're right," he said softly, "nothing could literally happen to him if I gave his name. But, you see, Senator McCarthy has no right to ask these questions of me or anyone else. No right." He sank back on the couch. "He's trying to punish people for their ideas."

"But, Dad, Mr. Truett is *dead*. This way they won't send you to prison."

"What about Barbara Truett, Jamie? How do you think she'd feel if I named her father?" Dad rubbed his forehead. "How would you feel if Uncle Joe's name was in an ugly headline in tomorrow's newspaper? Don't you see?" he said. "It wrongs the person, dead or alive. It sullies his memory."

I sat frozen.

"It would be a betrayal of all I believe in. And I believe in our democracy." He sighed.

I stared at him. "Democracy doesn't get fingerprinted and sleep in a prison cell, but you will."

"When we lose the right to think for ourselves, we are all behind bars. Democracy is not just an idea. We breathe life into it by living it."

I started to cry. "You don't care about anything but your precious democracy. You don't care about us!"

I ran back into my room. A little while later I heard Dad walk down the hall into his and Mom's room.

THE LAST few days at school have been a blur. My *NB* assignment isn't due yet, which is good because I'm a mess. Mrs. Ridit has left me alone, but not Charlie. "They're gonna get your old man! They're gonna get him!" Stuff like that, in the hallways, in the yard, on the street.

I'm going to the library. I need to look up something about Machu Picchu. I've got it written down. I can't seem to remember anything, except that Dad's going to prison.

Dad's out a lot, and I'm glad. Ever since we argued

about Mr. Truett, I've avoided him as much as I can. If he sticks his head in my room, I stare at the page I'm reading and pretend not to know he's there. At the table I don't look at him. I don't want to think about him, because when I do, I picture him in a striped prison suit and hat, *real*-movies style. I don't have my own movie about him. I can't find an ending I like.

"Excuse me, Mrs. Finley?"

She came out of her office. "Yes, Jamie, what is it?"

She's not somebody you expect a hug from, but at least she doesn't bark at me anymore. I started to tell her I had to do research on the Incas, when she rushed out from behind the desk. "Jamie, what is it?"

I can't explain. Tears were running down my face. Mrs. Finley put her arms around me. She feels softer than she looks. Next thing I knew, we were sitting in her office.

"I'm really sorry . . . it's really stupid . . . I'm really sorry . . ."

"My dear, I really wish you'd stop saying 'really.'"

I cried some more.

"Is this about your father?"

I nodded. "I'm really scared he's going to go to prison."

Mrs. Finley handed me a tissue.

"Hi."

We both turned. Harriet was at the front desk.

"I thought you might be here," she said to me.

Mrs. Finley walked out from her office, and I followed. She headed for an empty table at the back of the reference section. Harriet was behind me.

When we were seated, Mrs. Finley looked at Harriet. "You understand all this, don't you, Harriet?"

Harriet nodded. "It happened to us, Jamie, and we're okay," she said. "I guess."

"I'm sure Jamie would like to hear any details you want to tell her," Mrs. Finley said.

Harriet looked at me, and I looked down at my hands. "I feel like I'm going to explode inside," I said in a low voice. "And I can't figure out what to do." I looked at Harriet. "Did your father get called before the McCarthy committee?"

"No. An education committee of the university. They read things off a piece of paper and said he was fired."

"Was it on television?" I asked.

She shook her head.

"Senator McCarthy's on television. So the whole world will see my dad."

The wall clock ticked.

"That's awful," Harriet said. "But maybe he'll be lucky. Maybe he'll get to say something. At least stand up for himself." She blushed. "The hardest part was seeing my dad so defeated."

I can't picture Dad defeated.

Mrs. Finley coughed.

"My dad keeps saying we have to defend democracy, but democracy isn't going to go to prison." I could barely hear my own voice. "My grandma says it's not about fancy words, but people."

"I see," Mrs. Finley said.

I started to cry again.

"Why don't you bring your grandmother to the library one day, Jamie. I'd like to meet her."

Grandma and Mrs. Finley. That stopped my crying.

Harriet and I looked at each other. She was probably thinking about her father. I know I was thinking about Dad.

"Mrs. Finley, what's going to happen to my dad?" I said.

Mrs. Finley looked at Harriet. "Did your father get another job?" she said.

"He's a sales representative for a paint and flooring company."

I stared at Harriet. "Does he like it?"

"I'm not sure. He says he misses talking with his students." She shrugged. "I guess it's better than no job at all."

Mrs. Finley rose from her seat. "You two may stay back here and talk if you'd like." She turned and walked to the front desk. Her hair was pinned up in a bun, like Grandma's. I'd never noticed that before.

WHEN I left the library, I cut across Mayfair Avenue. Uncle Maury was just coming out of the subway station, and we walked home together. "Hey, Jamie," he said. Before I could say anything, he started to talk about Dad, nonstop. We took a detour around the playground at least three times.

"Your father joined the party because he thought the Communists were good people. I'm not sure how to help you understand."

"Mr. Stingypuss Pennypincher the Third?"

He looked surprised. "Many years since I've heard that." But he didn't smile. "The words 'social justice' and 'economic fairness' mean something very real, Jamie. If you think about it, every prophet in everybody's religion talks about that."

He scratched his head like Grandma. "Ha, listen to me. And you know what I think about both religion and the Communist Party. The real joke is, back in the thirties if a group of us were talking, I didn't always know what political party someone belonged to. When we argued, and we had whoppers of fights"—he paused and looked happy at the memory—"we shared something. We believed—I think the whole country believed—things could change, could get better. President Roosevelt did a lot to bring the country out of the Depression. And things did get better."

A sad note crept into his voice. "But something's missing now from political discourse."

"What?"

"Caring about others," he said. "You think that's corny, don't you?" He poked my arm.

"Not exactly."

"It's okay. Nothing wrong with corn. Besides, things will continue to change, and people will care again. They have to. Your father still does. And Uncle George, even though you know we disagree." He paused. "People will care again," he repeated wistfully.

Then he said something that made my brain shut down.

"You know, Jamie, in nineteen thirty-nine, before

you were born, Stalin and Hitler signed a war pact. Your father believed that nothing in the world justified joining with Hitler. And so he left the party."

Left the party! A century passed before I could say anything. I counted sidewalk squares—eight, eight and a half, "I didn't know that," nine, nine and a half—"Why doesn't he tell that to the McCarthy committee?"

One look at Uncle Maury's face and I knew the answer.

"It's none of their business," we both said at the same time.

But Dad's not a Communist anymore, I kept thinking. And there's Mr. Truett who's dead. Two ways Dad could be free, and he won't use either one.

I was supposed to read my history assignment after dinner, but I kept looking at Dad. He was making notes on a pad. He'd write something, then cross it out, then write more. His head was bent down, and two fingers of hair stood up in the back. Like Stevie. He was writing quickly. I couldn't see the paper, but I knew the words would be neat and the ink dark. Dad didn't skim lightly over a page. He pressed hard.

"It wrongs the person, dead or alive," he had said. "It sullies his memory. And it would be a betrayal of all I believe in."

Betrayal of all he believes in. He'd be free if he gave

Mr. Truett's name, but he wouldn't be living the way he wants to live.

Suddenly I got it. It would be like saying it was okay for the Stillwells to get kicked out of their apartment, or for Charlie to call Annie Mae a nigger. Or for Dad's school to fire him for something that had nothing to do with his teaching math.

I felt a rush of love.

There's more strange stuff. I'm still going all the way to Mrs. Manny's for the newspapers, even though nothing's a secret anymore. The other day I picked up the *Daily Worker*, along with the regular papers. Dad had said, "If I want to read the Communist Party paper, nobody will stop me, not the Board of Education, not Senator McCarthy." I carried the papers folded up inside the *Herald Tribune* for four blocks before I realized what I was doing. I unfolded them. My heart began to race, but I held them, face front, just like that, under my arm.

Some things don't change, like Mrs. Baumgarten. My friend. If there's a line at the bakery counter when I come in, she always takes me first. She says to the other customers, "Don't worry, no favorites. This little girl was here before." She doesn't smile and I don't smile. We both pretend I was there before.

Then there's Mom's friend, Mrs. Mandel. She was walking toward me one afternoon as I was coming home from the grocery store. When I said hi, she crossed to the other side of the street. Wait till Dad goes to prison. Mrs. Mandel will probably move out of the state just to steer clear of us. I wish Henry Taylor, Gail Boseman, Charlie, and every other miserable rat would go with her.

"Are you scared, Jamie?"

I was opening my locker. When I turned, Elaine said, "I'd be. Listen, I . . . I'm sorry." Then she left for class.

During recess, she was standing alone by the fence. I went over. "You should've told me," she said. "I mean, we were friends. You should've told me."

"I couldn't," I said. "You hate politics, and your father . . . well, I just couldn't."

She ran her fingers over the fence. "Yeah, well, Gail Boseman asked me questions about you. And when I started to tell her, I felt weird." She shrugged. "So I stopped. Don't worry. I never mentioned the Fettlesons. I promised you that." She kicked at the gravel.

It felt like the sun was shining inside my chest. A whole life ago Elaine stopped being my friend, but today we're talking again.

"You'd like my grandma," I said.

Then, at exactly the same moment, we both said, "My dad said . . ."

"You go first."

"No, you."

"My dad said your father will go to prison, and that he deserves it." She bent over to pick up a pebble. She held out her hand. The stone was brown, with light-gray wavy lines, and she gave it to me.

"I didn't like when he said that. He told me I'm not supposed to talk to you anymore." We were both silent for a minute. "But he didn't make me promise."

Then I told her that what her father had said about prison was probably true. I explained about the First Amendment, and how Dad wasn't even in the Communist Party anymore, and how he wasn't going to name any names, and that it all really scared me.

"He's brave," she said. And I knew that was the right word.

"I'm sorry I ever even talked to Gail Boseman," she said.

"I did once too." We both stared at the gravel. I picked up a rock a lot like the brown one and gave it to her. Then I told her about my plan about Mr. Truett, and how Dad wouldn't do it.

She nodded as if she understood both of us.

I took out my peanut butter and jelly sandwich and gave her half.

"Remember how you didn't tell Mrs. Ridit on me about the Gregory Peck picture?" she said. "Isn't that the same thing? Not naming names?"

I stared at her. "You're right to like Paul," I said. "And he's not just serious."

She smiled shyly. "Maybe I'll eat with you guys in the caf tomorrow."

When I got home, Uncle George was there with Grandma.

"Your father is with the lawyer," Grandma said.

"Come sit down." Uncle George motioned to me.

I sat at the table and waited.

"Jamie, look at me." He peered at me head-on. His eyes were magnified by his glasses. I hadn't known they were blue-green, like mine.

"I won't try to explain anything, Jamie. But know this," he said. "To be able to listen to your own voice above all the shouting, that is the mark of a special person. My brother, your father, is such a person."

I studied Uncle George's face. I'd known him all my life, but I felt like I was meeting someone new, someone I could actually talk to, maybe.

"He's going to go to prison," I said.

"There are worse things," he said. "Betrayal, for one."

And for the second time today, I knew that was the right word.

DAD TESTIFIES before the McCarthy committee late this afternoon. The hearing is downtown. Mom wanted to go, but Dad said he didn't want any of us exposed to the rapacious media. I didn't look it up. I got the idea.

"You're shutting me out, Pete, and it hurts," Mom said.

Dad looked pained. "Senator McCarthy is brilliant at twisting people's words and pounding witnesses until they break. I'm not going to break. But, Rachel, you of all people understand the media. The radio microphones and television cameras will also be turned on you."

"I don't care," Mom said.

"Of course you do. Can't you see the headline? WEEPING WIFEY CRACKS UNDER PRESSURE AS McCARTHY STEAMROLLS OVER HUBBY."

Mom smiled, and then began to laugh. She rocked back and forth laughing so hard she was crying. Dad got up and held her.

We don't have a television, but Barry's mother invited us down to watch on their set. I haven't talked to Barry since all this started, and I'm scared to watch Dad. Will they handcuff him right there with the whole world watching? We're all going down, me included, ready or not.

I was the last one in, behind Aunt Sheila. I heard Barry telling his mother that the Morses and Israels had arrived. We were an invading army, enemy occupiers, I'm sure, to an un-friend like Barry.

I sat at the dining room table at the far end of the living room, facing the television. Everybody else sat in the chairs and on the couch close to the screen. Barry came over to the table. I wasn't going to talk to him. He offered me a Three Musketeers bar, and without thinking, I said, "Thanks."

He sat down across from me. "My mom says your dad's doing a tough thing." Barry clapped his hands and snapped his fingers. He does that whenever he wants you to know he's said something important. I hadn't realized I'd missed seeing him clap and snap. I smiled, and he clapped and snapped again.

Senator McCarthy banged his gavel on the table-top and called the room to order. His voice is oily and gravelly at the same time. He had a stack of papers in front of him and *he was holding up a file. Same as the library picture.*

"There's Dad!" I said. He had come through the back door into the hearing room, and the television cameras followed him as he walked down the center aisle. He took a seat at the table facing Senator McCarthy. He sat straight up.

"Raise your right hand," the senator said. "Do you swear to tell the truth . . ."

Words swirled around. I heard Senator McCarthy say, "Sir, are you now, or have you ever been, a member of the Communist Party?"

"I choose not to answer you," Dad said. "A truth I hold to be self-evident is that my political beliefs are my business alone."

"Sir, there'll be no soapbox pronouncements in this room," Senator McCarthy said. He pointed to the man sitting next to him. "My chief counsel here, Roy Cohn, will explain the protocol." He leaned back in his seat and scratched his cheek.

"Mr. Morse," Roy Cohn began, "this is an official

Senate hearing, as I'm sure you understand." He went on as if he were lecturing a fourth-grader. "You must answer the questions as you would in a courtroom. You are at risk of contempt."

Dad smiled ever so slightly. "Indeed, sir, contempt I have," he said.

Senator McCarthy leaned forward. "We know you're a Communist, Mr. Morse. We don't need confirmation from you. We are merely giving you a chance to come clean."

"There is nothing clean about this hearing," Dad said.

"I'll ignore that, Mr. Morse. Now, when you went to meetings with Mr. Henry Taylor, there were others present."

"Senator, perhaps I didn't make myself clear. If I will not speak about my politics, surely I will not speak about other people."

"You're damaging your case, Mr. Morse. These are treacherous times, but believe me, we will root out every one of you!" McCarthy grinned and pounded the table. "We don't need you, Mr. Morse. You need us. No more games, Mr. Morse. We want names."

"Actually," Dad said, "you are quite correct in your desire for names. And I'm happy to give you a few."

"What's happening?" I grabbed Mom's arm.

Dad leaned forward in his chair. The hearing room was silent. And so was Mrs. Tollman's living room.

"Certainly I can name names of people who are determined to undermine the Constitution."

Senator McCarthy smiled. "I thought you'd come around."

"Among them, sir," Dad said, "you and your chief counsel Roy Cohn. You both are inflicting serious damage on the body politic and on the principles of our Constitution."

"That's enough!" the senator growled.

But Dad went on. "Your committee and the other Congressional committees, in your search for so-called subversives, have ignored precisely what has made this nation great—"

"That will be enough!" McCarthy was shouting by now.

"—the multiplicity of voices, the differing ideas, the dialogue—"

Uncle George pointed at the television screen. "They can't stop him! Look at that! He's magnificent!"

Dad was standing now.

Senator McCarthy shouted, "That'll be enough, mister," but still Dad kept on.

"As a great American once said, Senator, 'You may fool all the people some of the time; you can even fool some of the people all the time; but you can't fool all of the people all the time.' And your bleak time, sir, is coming to a close."

"Guards!"

"You want clean sheets to sleep in, sir. So do we all."

"I love you, Pete!" Mom said to the television.

"Leave this room now, Mr. Morse, or I'll have you . . ."

"You like a nourishing meal, don't you, Senator? So do we all."

"Guards! Take this man!"

"Congratulations, Senator, on your recent marriage. Should you have children, I hope you can afford their doctor's bills, for surely . . ."

"Will you be silent!"

"And for your children, sir, I know you'll want peace in this world."

Two guards pulled Dad away from the table.

Catch a tiger by the toe.

People were shouting in the hearing chamber. No one said a word in the living room. The news announcer came on to say the hearing was adjourned. And Barry's mother turned off the television.

Nobody said a word for several minutes. Then Grandma sat forward in her chair. She pointed to the screen, then turned to me and said, "Politics do not come to you through mother's milk. You choose who you become." She pointed again at the television. "Be proud."

I think I am.

Two nights after the hearing, Mom opened several bottles of wine, borrowed Mrs. Tollman's electric coffeepot, filled ours up as well, and sent me to Mrs. Baumgarten's for four dozen rugalach. She invited friends and family over. People crowded into our apartment. I knew some, like Mrs. Baumgarten. Lots I didn't.

I guess we all still had friends. I invited Harriet, Mrs. Finley, and Elaine. I knew Elaine wouldn't be able to come, but Mrs. Finley and Harriet did. I could even have a club. Me and Elaine and Harriet, and Herbie and Brian and Paul, if we let in boys. Maybe even Barry. In between chomping down on cookies, Barry was talking to Harriet, and she was listening.

People slapped Dad on the back, made jokes, got into political discussions. Nobody seemed to be thinking about the fact that he is going to prison in two months. His trial for contempt of Congress is scheduled then, and he will be convicted. We all know that.

I went into my room and sat on the bed in the dark. Stevie came in and sat with me for a while, then left. I could hear Uncle Maury and Uncle George arguing, but it sounded like they were enjoying themselves.

Dad is brave, like Uncle Joe. And I know I was wrong about Mr. Truett. But Dad's going to prison.

"Hey, pickle-puss." Dad hasn't called me that since I was seven or eight. He closed the door behind him and sat down next to me. He hugged me.

I've got an ending. The camera moves along the barbed-wire fence. The Crazy Lady is at the gate, waiting to meet Dad when he's released. She's got a million dollars in one-dollar bills in that shopping bag she always carries. "Family is family," she says as she hands him a fistful of money. She takes his arm and says, "And normal is whatever we are."

NOTE TO THE READER

I was a young teenager during the McCarthy period, but *Catch a Tiger by the Toe* is not my family's story. Jamie is a fictional character whose world was turned upside down in the summer and fall of 1953.

After the Depression and World War II, the 1950s seemed comfortable for many Americans. But it is also true that something dark happened. It was a time when the fear of Communism gripped the country.* Caught in the hunt for Communists, thousands of Americans were accused of being "Red" or political leftists.

In European democracies, leftist political parties operated side by side with other parties, and were part of the

---

*Communism is a complex economic and political system. But the basic idea is that the government would control what a society produces and that the wealth of a society would be shared by all workers, with no very rich or very poor people. Many feared not only communist ideas, but also that the Soviet Union, the first country controlled by a communist party and run by a powerful totalitarian government, would try to take over the world.

national political debate. In America, however, although the parties were legal, laws were passed that made it extremely difficult to be a Communist or Socialist. People were hounded if they joined the parties, or even if they were friends with someone who was a member. And since these parties were working, for example, to end racial segregation, many people were afraid to become involved in civil rights for fear of being labeled a "Red."

Thousands lost their jobs and homes even though they had committed no crime. Some were persecuted because they had attended certain lectures or meetings, or had written letters to the editor. Others never knew why they were singled out.

Soon people became afraid to express their opinions. A great many were even afraid to have a conversation about politics. You never knew who might be listening. Dissent was called unpatriotic. Students at the University of Chicago even refused to sign a petition asking for a soda machine in a science lab, because they believed it was risky to sign their names to anything. It is hard today to imagine that such a fear could grip America. But it did, smack in the middle of the twentieth century.

The most famous "Red hunter" in the country was someone whose name you might not have known, Senator Joseph McCarthy. In the 1950s, however, the whole world knew who he was. He accused many people of un-American activities. Yet even though he was the number one "Red hunter," a leading biographer says he never actually found a single Communist. Still, he ruined many lives.

In televised Senate hearings in 1954 (after this story ends), millions of people across America had a chance to watch McCarthy in action, to see his bullying style, and they didn't like it. By the end of that year, he was no longer front page news, and the fear he had inspired began to dissipate. Today most people agree that terrible things happened to our democracy during the McCarthy period.

The senator left us a new word, "McCarthyism." Many people have called McCarthy a demagogue, a person who uses fear and prejudice to gain power. McCarthyism, President Truman said, "is the use of the big lie and the unfounded accusation against any citizen in the name of Americanism or security."

I interviewed many people who were in elementary and middle school during the 1940s and 50s, and who had lives similar to Jamie's in this story. They grew up in leftist families. But I don't think you have to know very much about Communism to understand this story. It is in large part about bullies, big and small, and one teenager's struggle to deal with her worlds—the secret one, the public one, and the one she needs to grow into.

P.S. Although this story is fictional, the names of politicians, movie actors, Hollywood producers, newspapers, and magazines are real, as are the quotations from *Time* magazine and *The New York Times*. And a proposed movie about Hiawatha *was* canceled for fear that the story of a "peacemaker" might be seen as leftist propaganda.

The execution of the Rosenbergs, charged with being spies

for the Soviet Union, also happened as described. At the time, millions of people around the world, like Jamie's family, believed the Rosenbergs were innocent. With information from newly-opened U.S. and Soviet government files, it now seems that Julius Rosenberg was involved in passing some information to the Soviets, although his wife, Ethel, was not. Without the Red-hunting hysteria of the time, however, it is unlikely that either of them would have been sentenced to death. But because of their trial, thousands of American leftists not involved in any espionage activities were nonetheless tarred with the label "traitor" and subjected to persecution by people like Senator McCarthy.

SUGGESTED READING

If you want to read more about the McCarthy period and the senator himself, here are some fine books.

Several of these books were written specifically for young people (marked YP); others are histories, biographies, memoirs, and collections of letters, which, although written for adults, offer fascinating chunks of history for the interested young reader. Each book details a piece of history as seen through the eyes of the particular author. Together they create a richly detailed picture of the period, and of Senator McCarthy and the world he maneuvered in, the skills he brought to his political battles, the effects of his Red-hunting campaigns, the role of other public figures, and the lasting consequences of what one author has called "the nightmare decade."

Adams, John G. *Without Precedent: The Story of the Death of McCarthyism*. New York: W.W. Norton & Co., Inc. 1983. (First-hand account of the Army-McCarthy hearings in 1954, written by the key army official involved in investigations.)

Chambers, Whittaker. *Witness*. New York: Random House, 1952. (Book by the former Communist who was the prime accuser and witness against Alger Hiss.)

Cohen, Daniel. *Joseph McCarthy: The Misuse of Political Power*. Brookfield, Conn: The Millbrook Press, 1996. (YP; biography)

Cook, Fred J. *The Nightmare Decade: The Life and Times of Senator Joe McCarthy*. New York: Random House, 1971. (Passionate, but occasionally sloppy, particularly with dates.)

Denenberg, Barry. *The True Story of J. Edgar Hoover and the FBI*. New York: Scholastic, 1993. (YP; biography of the man and the institution.)

Hiss, Tony. *The View from Alger's Window: A Son's Memoir*. New York: Knopf, 1999. (A loving and respectful memoir by Alger Hiss's son.)

Ingalls, Robert P. *Point of Order: A Profile of Senator Joe McCarthy*. New York: G.P. Putnam's Sons, 1981. (YP; biography.)

Kahn, Albert E. *The Game of Death: Effects of the Cold War on Our Children*. New York: Cameron & Kahn, 1953. (Stories about children, schools, and parents, living in a time of national fear.)

Kaplan, Judy, and Linn Shapiro, eds. *Red Diapers: Growing Up in the Communist Left*. Champaign: University of Illinois Press, 1998. (Fascinating collection of essays by children of leftist parents.)

Matusow, Harvey. *False Witness*. New York: Cameron & Kahn, 1955. (Recanting by a former anti-Communist who had been a secret informer for government agencies.)

McGilligan, Patrick, and Paul Buhle. *Tender Comrades: A Backstory of the Hollywood Blacklist*. New York: St. Martin's Press, 1997. (Collection of interviews with those who were blacklisted in Hollywood.)

Mishler, Paul C. *Raising Reds: The Young Pioneers, Radical Summer Camps, and Communist Political Culture in the United States*. New York: Columbia University Press, 1999. (Study of schools and camps for children of leftist parents. More academic than most.)

Navasky, Victor S. *Naming Names*. New York: Viking, 1980. (Powerful study of the process and effects of the government's Red-hunting Congressional committees. Many original interviews.)

O'Brien, Michael. *McCarthy and McCarthyism in Wisconsin*. Columbia: University of Missouri Press, 1980. (Study of McCarthy's beginnings, his roots. Includes the real story of McCarthy's military service.)

Oshinsky, David M. *A Conspiracy So Immense: The World of Joe McCarthy*. New York: The Free Press, Macmillan, 1983. (Considered one of the leading biographies of Senator McCarthy.)

Reeves, Thomas C. *The Life and Times of Joe McCarthy: A*

Biography. New York: Stein and Day, 1982. (Another major biography.)

Rovere, Richard H. *Senator Joe McCarthy.* New York: Harcourt, Brace, Jovanovich, 1959. (Historian Arthur M. Schlesinger, Jr. called this "a brilliant essay in contemporary history.")

Schrecker, Ellen. *Many Are the Crimes: McCarthyism in America*, Boston: Little Brown, 1998. (Rich and detailed material. Schrecker is one of the major historians of the McCarthy era.)

Stone, I. F. *The Haunted Fifties.* New York: Random House, 1963. (A collection of Stone's articles and essays throughout the decade.)

Trumbo, Dalton. *Additional Dialogue: Letters of Dalton Trumbo 1942–1962.* Ed. Helen Manfull. New York: M. Evans and Co., 1970. (Wonderful collection of letters about life and politics and art.)

_____.*The Time of the Toad: A Study of Inquisition in America, and Two Related Pamphlets.* New York: Harper & Row, 1972. (Powerful indictment of the assault on the First Amendment.)

ACKNOWLEDGMENTS

I am ever grateful to those who told me their childhood secrets, and to my sisters Mada Liebman and Dori Brenner, my childhood partners with whom I share a world of memories. I'm particularly indebted to Anne Koedt, Miriam Cohen, and Jane Resh Thomas, early believers in this book, even when I faltered. My colleagues on the faculty of Vermont College's MFA program in writing for children and young adults and my New York City circle of writer friends were, as always, wonderfully supportive.

Finally, this book would not have come to life without Jill Davis's belief that this story should be told. For that I am most beholden.